THE
ANSWER

*How to Get the Best Answers to
Your Life's Biggest Questions*

JANE LEE

Pure Lee
PUBLISHING

ISBN 978-1-7781931-0-1 (paperback)
ISBN 978-1-7781931-1-8 (e-book)

BISAC: SEL031000 SELF-HELP / Personal Growth / General. | OCC019000 BODY, MIND & SPIRIT / Inspiration & Personal Growth. | SEL032000 SELF-HELP / Spiritual

Cover design by Jane Lee & Marigold W.

CONTENTS

The Answers Within

AT THIS VERY moment, there are millions of people—perhaps like you—contemplating life-changing questions. *Should I quit my job? Should I end my relationship? Should I move?* Maybe you've ruminated over your question for months, if not years, all the while slowly feeling more stuck or unsatisfied as time passes. You may have felt as though you should be satisfied with what you have, that you should just be grateful, that it all should be enough. But deep down, there is a feeling, a small knowing, that something isn't right. You may have tried to suppress or rationalize it, but doing so only makes it harder—and perhaps more painful—to ignore. If you're looking for ways to work through it, to find your answers, and to feel better, then you've picked the right book. Welcome.

You may have been drawn to this book if you're feeling lost or are seeking validation. When faced with a critical decision, people often have an inkling of what the right answer is for themselves; however, they are resistant, living in fear. Afraid of making the wrong decision. Afraid of taking a risk. Afraid of doing something new. Afraid of what others will think. Afraid of the consequences. Afraid of the unknown. *The Answer* will help you get the best answers for your questions, but it's much more than that. It's a guide that provides tools and practices to get you more attuned to your inner wisdom, so that when any question arises, there can be a deep knowing and foundation that everything will be fine. That all is—and will be—well. This book will help you build a connection to the inner faith you may need to always make the best decision for yourself, with confidence. To give yourself permission to live in your truth.

**The Answer will share how to get the best answers
to your most important life questions.**

I'll outline the steps anyone can take to gain more clarity and peace of mind in addressing the questions you face, and uncovering the answers you've been looking for. Instead of continuously searching for advice, validation, and answers from external sources and experts, you'll learn to look within and ultimately trust yourself. I'll walk through the steps, tools, and practices that will help connect you to your inner wisdom, and guide you to your best answers for critical questions.

My Journey to The Answer

In 2019, I was blindsided by a colon cancer diagnosis while pursuing fertility treatments and trying to conceive a second child. That very same day, just an hour later, I also got a call letting me know that the corporate dream job I'd been targeting for the last eight months—and had worked a lifetime to achieve—was finally offered to me. I was in shock and agreed to come in the following week for meetings and didn't mention anything about the diagnosis. After I got off the phone, I looked up toward the sky. I felt like the universe was giving me a clear message: choose your health or your career.

The cancer diagnosis hit me hard out of the blue. I felt like I had been sideswiped by a car. I didn't fit the typical profile of a colon cancer patient. I was 38 years old, a non-smoker, non-drinker, at a healthy weight, ate well, and exercised. I taught yoga part-time and was conscious of eating organic, whole foods. In an instant, I went from fertility clinic waiting rooms surrounded by women, to the hospital waiting rooms for my oncology appointments surrounded by fellow cancer patients who were senior citizens, and mostly male. And then there was me, a young mom.

But in hindsight, there were signs. There always are. They're just easier to see in the rearview mirror. I had first noticed blood occasionally in my stool in my early twenties. I remember telling my boyfriend (now husband) about it, and him telling me that it wasn't normal, and I should get it checked out. I wasn't concerned, but brought it up at my next annual physical with my doctor. She was an experienced physician, and I liked and trusted her. She said, "It's probably nothing — you're young, not overweight, don't drink, don't smoke and are healthy." I heard a similar refrain from doctors over the years before I was diagnosed about fifteen years later. At the time, my doctor told me that it was likely a hemorrhoid, and when I replied that I didn't have any, she said it was likely an internal one I couldn't see. I accepted that and left it.

Over the years, I noticed that my diet affected when I'd see blood in my stool, and I started reducing my dairy and wheat consumption. Whenever I indulged in dairy, I would inevitably get bloated and see blood again. My doctors didn't think there was a connection, but clearly, my body was trying to tell me something. For someone who had aspired to be a professional ice cream taste tester as a child, it wasn't easy to cut out dairy. Whenever people questioned why I was limiting or not consuming cheese, I always said that while I loved the taste of cheese, cheese didn't love me. It took me years to get to a place where I regularly avoided dairy in my diet, save for the occasional exception. Total elimination wasn't in my vocabulary. Coming from a large Chinese family, food is life. My grandfather always told me it was better to eat mindfully and allow myself little bit of everything, than to declare I would never eat a certain item again.

When my physician retired, I found a new one available in my neighbourhood. During our first appointment, we went over my general medical history, of which I relayed to her that I had blood in my stool once in a while, and briefly summarized my previous doctor's response to it. At that point, it had already been about fifteen years since I first noticed it. My new physician said it was likely nothing, but it wasn't a normal thing, so, she referred me to a specialist. I had an appointment with the specialist, and he repeated the same refrain I had heard from doctors before him, "You're young, healthy, not overweight, don't smoke, don't drink, it's probably nothing," but he suggested I have a colonoscopy to check everything out and ensure there was nothing there. He also explained that while small, there were risks with colonoscopies and said it was 95% likely there was nothing wrong with me. A couple of weeks after that appointment, I canceled the scheduled colonoscopy, thinking there couldn't be anything wrong, and with my busy schedule, I reasoned it was easier this way.

Fast-forward later that year to when I sat in my fertility doctor's office. He was the third fertility doctor I'd seen in the last seven years. Over the years, they had eliminated any of the obvious reasons as to why we had difficulty conceiving (we had what was called "unexplained infertility"). He theorized that I perhaps had endometriosis, and suggested I see another specialist regarding a procedure to remove it if present. As part of my fertility treatments, I would have regular cycle monitoring ultrasounds to help assess when it was best to have intercourse. During one of those regular ultrasound appointments, the technician noticed a mass in my colon and made note of it. By that point, I had already undergone many routine ultrasounds during my years in and out of fertility clinics, as it was one of the most standard procedures. I'd probably had at least 50-100 ultrasounds prior to that one, and that was the first time someone had noted anything about a mass in my colon, which they just happened to notice when they were moving the ultrasound wand over from one ovary to the other. Never the passive patient, I always reviewed all the notes and reports in my file, and when I inquired about it, I was told I had to talk to the doctor about the mass. So, there I was, sitting in his office a few days later. It was during this appointment that my doctor explained that he suspected I had endometriosis, which was common to wrap around the colon. When I questioned why the technician had noted it was a mass *inside* my colon and not *around* it, he said the ultrasounds were not always accurate, but there was no reason to suspect anything otherwise because I was "young, healthy, not overweight, didn't smoke or drink." Endometriosis could be confirmed through a laparoscopic procedure, which would also be used to laser the endometriosis away at the same time. He suggested that I first get the colonoscopy that I held off on earlier in the year before my appointment with the specialist regarding endometriosis, so she could have any applicable information needed. And so, one year after my first cancelled colonoscopy appointment was scheduled, I finally went in for the procedure. I didn't think much of it, just that it was something I needed to do before laparoscopy for endometriosis, which was going to be done before another round of IVF to try to have a second child. Things unfolded very differently than I expected.

When I awoke from the colonoscopy, I looked at the clock and noticed that an hour had passed versus the thirty minutes they said the procedure would take. The doctor told me that they found and removed four polyps. One in particular was fairly large and looked abnormal, so, it was sent for a biopsy. They assured me it was probably nothing, but they said they'd let me know the results in a couple of weeks. When I didn't hear back in that timeframe, I called the doctor and she suggested I come into the hospital to talk about my results. Naively, I still didn't really think anything of it. I worked from home that Friday morning with plans to see the doctor in the afternoon.

While I was working, I got an abrupt call from the hospital that startled me. "Is this Jane? I'm calling to schedule you for a CT scan on Sunday morning." I numbly finished the call and then dialed my husband at work and started crying, telling him what had just happened. Obviously, something was wrong. He came home right away and accompanied me to the hospital. The doctor told us both that the abnormal polyp she removed had tested positive as cancerous. Just like that, I got the diagnosis of colon cancer. Waves of shock, sadness, and disbelief came over me.

How was this possible? How could I have cancer? Me? But I feel fine. I look fine. But I'm so young. I'm so healthy. I don't smoke or drink. I have a young child. This isn't possible. How could this be?

That afternoon, I also got the news that after months of meetings and discussions, the VP position I had been interviewing for was finally offered to me. They wanted to move forward and asked me to come in for a few meetings on Tuesday. I agreed. Still in shock, I wasn't sure how to proceed with my regular life. I felt like the universe was giving me a very clear sign and asking, "*What are you going to choose, your health or your career?*" I had no idea what to do.

We already had plans for some of my cousins to come over that night for dinner. My husband asked me what I wanted to do, and whether I wanted to cancel. I shook my head, determined to move forward with our plans. I wasn't dying at that moment, so why not have dinner together? *Why should anything change?* That evening, when one of my cousins asked if I was still buying organic foods, I nodded and shared that I would be buying a lot more because I had just received a colon cancer diagnosis. A wave of hugs and tears fell over the room. It was fine, I told everyone, I'm okay.

I wasn't fine though. Things had drastically changed, and yet they hadn't. From discussions with the doctors, I learned I could've had the cancer for years without knowing, which made the whole diagnosis even harder to digest.

Over the following week, I continued experiencing waves of sadness, shock, and disbelief. And then one morning, I woke up, and everything felt very clear. I truly felt that everything was going to be fine. In fact, I *knew* it would be. I sat up in bed and told my husband, "It's going to be fine. I'm going to be fine. It'll all be okay." I just *knew*.

Months later, a lot had changed. I was healing and taking things slowly. I was meditating daily, and in one of my meditation sessions, I had an amazing experience where I felt myself spontaneously go back and tell my old self that everything would be fine—the old self that had awoken that day with the knowing that all would be well. At that moment, I realized that *I* had been the one to tell myself that it was all going to be okay. While I didn't fully understand it at the time, I had tapped into an internal wisdom. A greater intelligence than my human self that helped guide me then and continued to guide me throughout the whole process—and even to this day.

We can find our answers in so many places. While I had the feeling that everything would be fine, I was still dealing with the decision of what to do next in terms of treatment after receiving the diagnosis. The oncologist and my family all wanted me to undergo immediate surgery. In an appointment with the surgi-

cal oncologist, I asked him what my options were, and he drew
me a decision tree:

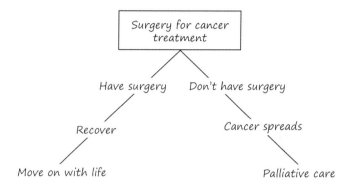

I understood right away that he meant death when he said
palliative care. With tears forming in my eyes, I asked, "These
can't be my only two options, can they?" He apologized for
being so blunt, but this was simply the way he saw the situation unfolding. Surgery would come and go, and then it'd be
a blip in my memory. But if I didn't do it, it would point to
certain death. I refused to believe that. I felt that I could heal
myself naturally; however, that option frightened most of my
family. My husband, ever supportive and loving, said that it was
completely up to me, and asserted that he'd support me in any
choice I made. In researching alternative approaches to healing, I watched a documentary called *Heal* that inspired me. My
siblings, however, had a different reaction after their viewing,
feeling angered that people were given what they called "false
hope." But I saw things differently.

The decisions I made during that pivotal time in my life were nothing I ever would have predicted. I not only healed and thrived after cancer on my own terms, but also took my career in an entirely new direction. I quit my six-figure salaried corporate job and turned down what I had once thought was my ideal executive job in the process—and I've never been happier, nor have I ever been more at peace.

The Answer is a culmination of my work and journey—the knowledge I've accessed, learned, and digested. It is what I teach to people every day through yoga, meditation, life coaching, mentoring, parenting, and by simply living my truth. The journey to getting the best answers will take time and effort, but I promise, if you practice the steps outlined and integrate these tools into your daily life, you will achieve greater clarity and peace of mind. For me, the process didn't always lead to the easy answers, nor the answers that others wanted me to choose, but *they felt right*. And those answers led to experiences and situations I never would have had otherwise, like sharing my story out loud with hundreds of people, or writing this book. In the chapters ahead, I'll share the steps I used, and how anyone can apply them to establish the foundation for the best answers to their own life's critical questions. Each chapter will walk through one of the steps I used—and continue to use—to help guide me to make the best decisions for myself. As I embarked on my journey, science and research helped me trust in the process, and as I progressed, I started trusting in the experience, myself, and the unknown. You'll see a similar journey in *The Answer* with scientific research and studies supporting the steps, and as the chapters progress, the process becomes more esoteric, and about tuning within.

You are at the Helm

This process of navigating to your best answers within is helmed by your best teacher: yourself. You are your own best teacher, guide, coach, and consultant. You know what you've been through, and are best equipped to figure out where you want to go and how to get there. I'm simply here to help, to be one of the many teachers and lights on your journey as you travel down your path in life. With each chapter, *The Answer* will share tools and practices to connect you with your inner wisdom, along with how to pull all the work together and trust what you are feeling. The rest is up to you.

There is going to be effort and time involved, and if you're willing to take that on, it'll be one of the best investments you make. But you need to be willing to do the work, to put in the time and energy, and to show up for yourself, every day. However, I promise if you follow through with everything outlined, you will achieve greater clarity, peace of mind, and so much more. Reading this book is only the beginning. Take it one step at a time. This is not a race or a competition. Your journey in life isn't meant to be compared and contrasted against someone else's. Wherever you are is perfectly fine. No matter where you're starting from, you're never truly lost. Invest in yourself, one step at a time.

To that end, if you read something here that doesn't sit right with you, that's fine. You don't have to follow everything someone else tells you to. If there are some steps or exercises that don't feel right at this time, leave them alone. Conversely, as with anything in life, what resonates with you is for you, meaning that it's best to start with the parts that stand out for you. I encourage you to notice the words, sentences, chapters, and actions that speak to you the loudest—the ones that pop and resonate. Those are the ones to pay attention to first. There is no correct order in which to do things; everyone is different, and everyone will take a different path. Just ensure that whatever you choose to do feels right. As you continue in your journey, you'll find that what resonates with you may change over time, especially as you evolve and delve deeper. You may find that if you revisit it later, some things that didn't make sense or feel right before feel differently now.

As you read through this book and start practicing the steps, you may find that you don't need to undertake all of them to get the answer you're looking for. Perhaps you're able to get attuned to your answer after learning how to better connect to your body and intuition (Chapter 2), and you feel that you've landed on the right decision just by using that. Or after creating your compass as outlined in Chapter 1, and starting a regular meditation practice (Chapter 3) coupled with journaling (Chapter 4), you feel at peace with your direction and are comfortable with the answers you need in your life. Whatever number of steps you choose to undertake to get to your answer is perfectly fine. Some of you may only need to try a handful of the steps to get an answer, while others may need to implement them all for some time. This is your unique journey, and none of our paths are the same. Do what feels right for you. As long as you're putting in effort, you're progressing. That also means some days you may not feel like doing any of this work, and that's okay. Let yourself feel whatever you're feeling, but

I would encourage you to show up every day and put in your best effort.

If you do get the answer to the question you're looking for without needing to undertake all of the steps, then that's great. However, note that taking on more steps may help you access answers to questions you haven't asked yet. Understanding and regularly practicing all of the steps outlined here can help build a foundation that supports a sense of knowing that all is and will be well.

Your Answers

Getting the right answers isn't about predicting the future and exact details; rather, it's about determining the best choice or path for you to take at that moment. This may change over time because answers are not absolute. Change is a constant in life, and you are not the same person you were yesterday, last week, or last year. Couple that with free will, and you may find that as situations evolve, you may need to re-evaluate your answers. The important part is to start taking steps in a direction that feels right for you. You don't need to know the exact destination to start your journey to your answers. You'll feel it when you're off course, and can re-evaluate at any point.

Take away any fear of making the *wrong* decision. Remove the pressure you placed on yourself to make the *right* decision. There are no ultimate right or wrong answers. Judgement of your decision-making will not help and is not needed, so please leave it behind. Trust that whatever you decide is best for you at that time. Also, don't pressure yourself into making a decision you may not be ready for. *Take your time.*

You are your best guide, so, don't be quick to allow others to make or influence decisions for you. Own your free will and feel what's best for you. It may take time to validate your answer, as you may already know the answer, but are too afraid to admit it or face it. This might be because moving forward with a particular answer could disrupt your life routine, bringing you some semblance of discomfort, and you simply may not be ready to face that yet, and that's okay. However, try not to let fear stop you from moving forward and progressing—from trying something new and different—because you never know where it will lead you.

Fear doesn't stand in your way unless you allow it to. Fear is a perception; it doesn't have to be your reality. You may conjure stories in your head of what could go wrong if you try something new, but you can't predict the future, and you may end up imagining a scary "what if" for yourself. It's best not to feed the fear, and instead focus on the present—how you feel at this moment. Don't let fear stop you from taking a step in the direction that feels right.

After receiving my cancer diagnosis, I started on a journey of healing that involved inner work, including the steps outlined in this book. With self-reflection, I realized that I had been judgmental and critical of others, and also of myself. What we don't often realize is that the way we treat others is also the way we treat ourselves. That angry person yelling at the cashier or waiter probably talks to themselves with the same anger. They treat others with anger because they are angry at themselves. It doesn't make it right, but it gives us more insight on our emotions and the impact of our choices. By being better to ourselves, we in turn treat others better. What does this have to do with getting the answers you want in your life? When you treat yourself and others with kindness, the world will open for you. The noise of criticism, anger, anxiety, and frustration will dim to reveal wisdom within. When you connect within, you will get a better sense of what to do when a question arises. Your inner guidance will become easier to access.

Often, it's straightforward for us to give advice and see the right path for friends and loved ones when they're at a crossroads or facing a dilemma. We want the best for them, which makes the answer obvious to us. Yet when we're the ones facing the dilemma and decision-making, it can feel harder. We may feel the answer is not as obvious because we convince ourselves it's complicated. We layer on a bunch of erroneous factors and fears that ultimately make it more difficult to choose the best decision for ourselves. But if we step back and look at the question with a loved one in our shoes instead (especially our child, niece, or nephew), the answer can often become clearer because it stems from a place of love rather than fear. Once we reinsert ourselves back into the picture, we tell ourselves it's more complicated than it seems, but it really isn't.

In the end, the answer is simply love. When you truly forgive, accept, and love your whole self with kindness, empathy, and compassion, the answers you seek will come easily. Life decisions will become less complicated when they are rooted in internal love. *The Answer* is an ideal place to start your journey toward this lifestyle. Let's get into it.

CHAPTER 1

Create Your Compass

We must be willing to let go of the life we planned
so as to have the life that is waiting for us.

Joseph Campbell

Finding Your Direction

To choose the right answers, it is extremely helpful to first know what direction you want to go in—or at least have a good sense of it. Once you know what you want out of life, you'll have a much easier time making decisions that are in your best interest, and ones that bring you closer to the life you want to live. For example, think about when you need to go out and buy groceries. Your starting point (i.e., your home, work, or someplace else), and where you want to buy the groceries (i.e., supermarket, local grocer) determine the direction and path you will take to get there. It's the same thing in life. Knowing your destination, like the grocery store—or in this case, how you want to live your life and feel—gives you a North Star or a goal post to indicate the path on which you should embark.

Once you know what kind of life you want to live, you'll have a much easier time making decisions that support your life direction. And it'll become more obvious when the path you've chosen is taking you further away from where you want to be. Defining how you want to feel and living your life accordingly can create a compass for your best answers. The right answers for you bring you closer to the life you want to live.

My Compass

When I was 25, I left the life I had known behind to embark on a new journey. I said goodbye to my job, friends, and family in Toronto—where I was born and raised—to have new experiences abroad. For months, I had felt an urge building within me to make a change, and I could no longer ignore it. While I had a good job, loving relationship, stable home, family, and friends, I wanted to experience something different. I wanted to stretch my boundaries and grow. I wanted to feel what it was like to be more independent, live somewhere else, and travel more. If I were single, I would have moved to another city for a couple of years to have that experience, but as I was in a committed relationship, and my then boyfriend (now husband) didn't want to leave his new job, I decided to go away on my own for six months instead. I knew I wanted to travel throughout Asia, and since I had always loved working with children, I found a volunteer role with a non-profit organization in China that cared for orphans with disabilities. I worked with them for a couple of months and fell in love with all the kids and babies I encountered. The first day I met the kids, I was taken aback. I wasn't used to seeing so many children who looked different, but that reaction quickly dissipated, and all I could see was how pure and loving each and every one of them was. They were just regular kids that were born a little different, and I grew to love them immensely. They found joy in their lives and had smiles on their faces, despite their circumstances, and I got so much joy from caring for and teaching them. It was hard to say goodbye.

During my time in China, I travelled around the country. On one particularly long solo train ride, I looked out the window for hours, watching the countryside pass by. I felt inspired to start writing down all the things I wanted to do, feel, and achieve in my life. I wrote and wrote and wrote, anything and everything that came to mind, and then I looked at it all. The list included travelling, volunteer work, spending time with friends and family, doing work I enjoyed, how I wanted to feel, how I wanted others to feel, and more. Then, I organically started grouping my answers together and distilled them, again and again, until I was left with just their essence. I found that I had outlined my three life goals on that paper, and it was really quite simple once I boiled it all down:

1. I wanted to be happy.
2. I wanted to be healthy.
3. I wanted to positively impact every person that crossed my path.

Fast forward a few years, entrenched back in the corporate working world in Toronto, I had strayed from my goals. While I had lost my way, I became focused on other plans instead of my life goals. My whole life I had been working to achieve. I wanted a six-figure salary, a director title, to be a homeowner, to get married, and to have my first child by the time I was thirty.

- ☑ six-figure salary
- ☑ director job title
- ☑ homeowner
- ☑ married
- ☐ child

Check, check, check, check, and *nope*. I learned that life could be painful when it didn't go the way you planned.

During this time, I was a director in a large digital agency with a heavy workload. I worked closely with the top executive, who seemed to live and breathe for work, and expected the same of others. I fell in line and found myself waking up early to work at home before going into the office, and then logging back on after dinner to work late into the night. One time, in a Women in Leadership group, I recalled our VP of HR responding to a question about work-life balance with an answer that she appreciated the flexibility of our company as she could attend her son's soccer games after work hours, and then work again at home until midnight. The culture was so ingrained in her that she didn't even realize that her answer wasn't well received. All that work left me with little time for anything else. My yoga practice and workouts had fallen by the wayside, and I rarely had time to relax. I allowed my free time to be consumed by work, and unsurprisingly, I was left feeling miserable. Outside of work, my husband and I had been trying to conceive unsuccessfully for a couple of years, and I knew my mental and physical health was suffering. I barely even saw my husband because I woke up early to work while he was still sleeping, and went to bed after he had already fallen asleep while I worked late into the night.

One day in bed, he looked over at me and shook me to my core with his words, "You used to be the one who always made me happy when I was sad, but now you're just always sad." I was heartbroken and shaken. How did I get here? I had the material trappings—a great title, salary, and career success—but at what cost? I clearly wasn't happy, wasn't healthy, and rarely spent time with the people I loved. On top of all that, I wasn't able to positively impact the person I loved most. Soon afterward, on a flight home during a work trip, I used the back of my boarding pass to analyze my two options: whether I should stay at my job or leave. I drew two columns, and in each column, I evaluated the options against my life goals of being happy, healthy, and positively impacting everyone who crossed my path. With tears streaming down my face, I looked at my boarding pass and knew that the answer was obvious.

Goals: To be happy. To be healthy. To have a positive impact on everyone who crosses my path. Question: Should I quit my job?			
Yes		No	
Pros	Cons	Pros	Cons
– less stress, more relaxed – healthier, more time to sleep, practice yoga, exercise – can find another job, done it before – supports and aligns with my life goals	– loss of income – walk away from a good job and title – career impact? unknown	– keep a steady and good income – career status quo	– remain stressed, unhappy and unhealthy – less quality time with Dave, friends and loved ones – doesn't support my life goals

I resigned with no other job lined up. I was burnt out and needed a break for my mental health before getting into the right headspace to look for my next role. I had always wanted to deepen my yoga practice and thought that it would be a good time to get more active again, so, I went right into Yoga Teacher Training after my last day of work. It was a shift on my path back toward my life goals, and little did I know how much I would get out of that turn. It didn't take me long to feel refreshed, happy, and healthy. Three months later, I started teaching yoga part-time as I enjoyed it so much, even though I had no intention of doing so before training. Meanwhile, as I continued to practice yoga and meditate daily, I was also actively looking to re-enter my corporate career. Soon after, I began interviewing for jobs, and while I was in the interview process, I found out I was pregnant. I had stopped going to the fertility clinic months earlier and became pregnant naturally when I was less stressed, happy, and healthy.

Since then, I've continued to use my life goals as a compass to help guide me in major decisions, to better align myself with the life I truly want, and notice if I have strayed from my path.

Creating Your Compass

When you clearly define what you want in life, what you want to do, and how you want to feel, it makes it much easier to answer life-changing questions as the right answers bring you closer to that life. Our lives on earth are short, and we don't know when our time is going to end. You may live to be over one hundred, or you may not make it to half that age. Use the time you have to live the life that you want, now. There's always a reason to wait until later before starting to fully enjoy your life, but what if that tomorrow doesn't come? What if the future you've worked toward and even suffered for your whole life doesn't arrive because your time on earth ended early? What if that future you've been working toward only lasts just one day, one week, one month, or one year? Will the way you have lived your life have been worth it? Would you have changed the decisions you made?

Bronnie Ware, bestselling author of *The Top Five Regrets of the Dying*, worked in palliative care for years. During that time, she had deep conversations with the people there and discovered their top regrets in life. There were commonalities amongst the stories she heard, and it culminated into her book, which outlined these top life regrets of the dying:

1. I wish I'd had the courage to live a life true to myself, not the life others expected of me.
2. I wish I hadn't worked so hard.
3. I wish I'd had the courage to express my feelings.
4. I wish I had stayed in touch with my friends.
5. I wish that I had let myself be happier.

Take a moment now to consider whether you relate to any of these regrets. What if you only had one month left to live? Would these regrets seem more palpable? If yes, are you willing to do something about it? Or will you keep waiting?

You have an opportunity right now—and every day—to choose the way you live, so that you have no regrets at the end of your life. Since our time on earth isn't promised, are you willing to put yourself first and prioritize your life? A good way to start is to figure out what kind of life it is you want to live. It is helpful to have quiet time alone to get a greater sense of what you enjoy doing in life and what you want for yourself, outside of the influence of family, friends, social media, and others. It's important to carve out time and space to be alone, unburdened by your day-to-day concerns so that you have time to reflect, think, feel, and contemplate. I understand that it may not be possible for all of you to take off on a solo vacation or retreat to do this, and you don't need to. But do the best you can to make and find pockets of time to be alone, still, and contemplative. To consider how you want to live and feel.

When I was on that long train ride alone in China, I thought about how I wanted to live my life, so that at the end of it, I would have no regrets. The exercise I completed helped me create my compass because when I was finished, I was left with my life goals in a neat and tidy list. Now it's your turn to do the same exercise.

The Work – Life Goals

I encourage you to complete this exercise when you have free time alone, are in a quiet space, and will be undisturbed. If you have time to settle in beforehand, that's ideal. You don't have to be on a vacation, but try to calm your mind before you begin. Find a way to center and relax yourself, be it with meditation, exercise, a walk, taking a bath/shower, and so on. Also, if it's accessible for you, doing this exercise in nature may be helpful, sitting by the water, in the woods, or in a park. However, don't wait for the perfect scenario to start; just take a few, slow, deep breaths, and get into it.

Imagine you are at the end of your life, sometime in the future. You understand and accept that you will be passing soon, with only a few days left to live. While your human body is slowly shutting down, your mind is still fully cognitive and alive. You reflect on your life and consider the following:

- How would you have wanted to live so that there are no regrets?
- What kind of life is it that you would've wanted to experience?
- How would you have wanted to feel in your life?
- Who would you have wanted to spend your precious time with?
- What would you have wanted to accomplish during your time on earth?
- How would you have wanted to spend your time?
- What would you have wished you had done?

Write down all the ideas and thoughts that come to mind. Don't try to filter yourself. This is about what you want, not what others will think or expect. You can use sticky notes (one idea or thought per note), or pieces of paper (one idea or thought per piece), or write them down one line at a time on a single sheet of paper, using as many as you need. You can also use a computer or smartphone to type it all out. However you choose to do it, just get all of it out and down.

When you're finished, look at your answers and start grouping related ideas and thoughts together. Consider what the essence is of the idea or thought. What is the impact after you've accomplished or completed it? Then, write a sentence or two that encapsulates the spirit of each group of answers. What is the headline for that group of ideas and thoughts? What will it mean at the end of your life?

Look at the sentences you've written for each group of answers. How do they feel? Sit with them if you need to for a while. Consider each one. Does it resonate with you as a life goal? How would you feel if you accomplished these goals by the end of your life? Feel free to make any edits and adjustments until they feel right.

Use your life goals as a compass to evaluate whether answers will bring you closer to your goals, or further away. Now, take a life question that has been on your mind. Look at the options for that life question, and evaluate the answers against your life goals. Which answer supports one or more of your goals? Which answer would detract you from your goals? The answer that supports your goals, and/or brings you closer to accomplishing them, are the ones that are likely best for you. The answers that detract from your goals may not be best for you. Your life goals are a compass for your best answers. The right answers for you bring you closer to the life you want to live.

Sometimes those answers may not be the easy answers, or you fear the potential consequences of pursuing the answer, even if you feel it's right for you. However, you don't know when your life on earth will end. So, how long are you willing to wait until you decide it's time to take a first step toward achieving these goals? Are you waiting for retirement, or when your kids are older? Are you waiting to become more financially stable? You can always find a reason to wait, but what if that "some day" never comes? Would you have regretted waiting, perhaps not even trying? There will always be reasons and excuses to justify why it's not the right time, why it's too late, or why it's too early, but there is never a perfect time. All you have is the present. The present is a gift, so use it wisely because there is no guarantee of tomorrow. Start now.

What steps can you take to get closer to your life goals? If you've figured out the best answer for yourself based on your compass that you've built out of your life goals, and you know deep down it's the right answer, what comes next? For some answers, it may be pretty straightforward—the hardest part having answered the question in the first place. However, if it feels impossible, lofty, or perhaps unachievable to reach or fulfill that answer, break it down. Break down the goals or answer into steps, and if needed, break down those steps even further until you get to a level that feels tangible and achievable. For example, perhaps you feel like changing careers, but that prospect seems daunting and overwhelming. Break it down into smaller steps. Some of the steps may include figuring out what you enjoy doing, researching career options of interest, enrolling in a course, and creating or revising your budget. If these steps still feel too difficult, break them down into even smaller steps. For example, telling yourself that you have to exercise an hour every day feels more daunting than setting an intention of doing five minutes of exercise daily. Break down the steps until they are achievable for you, and then build off them. As you start exercising, perhaps you'll feel like continuing after five minutes, or maybe add on another five minutes the next day. There are always steps you can take to get closer to fulfilling your answer and achieving your goals. Do not get lost or disheartened by how far away the goals may seem. Instead, focus on the next (small) step ahead of you.

Now, what would it feel like if you achieved what you were working toward, if you were living a life you love? Bring this feeling into your present life. This may involve creating vision boards, describing it in your journal, envisioning it in your mind, speaking like you already have it, repeating a mantra, and more. To help bring those goals and answers closer to you, start making decisions that help you feel the way you would if you achieved all the goals you set for yourself. When you are projecting those feelings, that energy will bring experiences that elicit those same emotions closer to you.

Goals versus Plans

The life goals you've defined can be used as a compass to guide you toward the answers that serve you best. Understand, however, that your life goals are not plans. Goals are different from plans. The path you take to reach your goal may be unexpected, because life doesn't always unfold the way we want it to. You may find, at times, that your life isn't going according to plan, which can be difficult. Try not to feel discouraged when things don't go as expected. It may be that those plans weren't right or best for you at that time, though it may not be obvious at that moment. There are many paths to take, and the one you set out for yourself isn't written in stone. Try to accept where you are because denying or fighting it doesn't change reality, and only serves to stagnate and stress you. Acceptance does not mean complacency. Once you can accept your position and the things that have happened, you can continue working toward your goals, while also allowing yourself to flow with what else may come your way. There may be turns on your path you didn't anticipate, but eventually get you to your goal. Allow yourself to be open to new and different things as you continue to strive for your goals, and you may find that things turn out even better than expected. The universe is supporting you and will reveal a path of least resistance to reach your goals, if only you are able to listen, tune in, and pay attention.

CHAPTER 2

Connect to Your Body & Intuition

There is more wisdom in your body
than in your deepest philosophy.

Friedrich Nietzsche

The One

LOOKING BACK ON my life, there were many times when I connected within and knew the answers instantaneously. In all my romantic relationships, I knew from the very first date whether we were going to last or not. I always saw—or rather *felt*—an end to relationships before the first date was even over, no matter how much chemistry and attraction there was. It was never because of anything they did or said. It was simply a sense, a knowing. When that knowing came, I told myself to simply have fun without expectations, although in the end, my intuition was invariably correct.

I met my husband at university while working on a group project together. Although I was attracted to him, I assumed

I wasn't his type, and when the school year ended, I thought we wouldn't see each other again. I was pleasantly surprised when he reached out, and even more surprised when we had an amazing first date together. Afterward, as I drove home alone, and just as I was getting onto the highway off ramp, I realized that this was the first initial date where I didn't *see* the end of a relationship. I suddenly started crying, which caught me off guard. We barely knew each other; however, knowing that he was "the one" made me burst into tears instantaneously, as I foresaw the challenges ahead with my family. While we were both children of Canadian immigrants—culturally, my family background is Chinese, while his is German—I knew my father wouldn't approve of me dating someone outside my race, and extended family members would gossip about me. Most of all, even though I wasn't sure how he'd react, I was worried about how my *ah gung* (grandfather) would react. All these thoughts and feelings ran through me, and just as quickly as they came, they passed as I made up my mind as I exited off the highway. *Let them talk*, I thought to myself. *If he's the one and we're happy together, let them talk.* I knew they would talk about us for a little while, then move onto the next topic of conversation, and I wasn't going to let that come between me and what felt right because what mattered was that I was happy. They wouldn't be spending their lives with him, I would.

Knowing he was the one, I told myself that if we made each other happy, we would be together, and we have been ever since. I was right about my family not approving; however, they all eventually came around, some sooner, and some later. There were two things that made them change their minds.

The first was when they met him, saw his face, and felt his presence. Although I knew my dad wasn't fully onboard yet, he was assuaged as he said Dave looked like a kind, old soul. Having gone through a previous relationship race issue with my mom, she now finally saw past colour, and just wanted me to be happy. As for my grandfather, my beloved *ah gung* whose reaction I was worried about the most, showed me I had nothing to fear. He had studied the *I Ching*, and knew how to accurately read people, their faces, and personalities. The first time he saw Dave, he told me that he was a loving, good-hearted, intelligent person, and gave me a thumbs up with a big smile. That was that. Sure, there were other family members who gossiped, but I realized that their reaction was more about them than it was about me. I had already decided I wasn't going to spend my energy and time worrying about them, and eventually, even they came around. They came around because of the second thing: Everyone—my family, friends, and even strangers in airports—noticed how much Dave loved and cared for me. He was always radiating kindness.

Your Bodies' Intelligence

Many of us look to outside sources for guidance when navigating personal questions; however, it is important to note that we are all connected to a deep wisdom and intelligence through our bodies that can help guide us to our best answers, if we know how to tap in. You can all tune into this intelligence and wisdom that some call intuition. Research demonstrates that our bodies are communicating with us and helping guide us. We just have to pay attention. The exercises outlined in this chapter will help you do just that.

Your body is more intelligent than you may know. It does so much. It keeps you breathing, your blood circulating, heart pumping, and regulates your temperature, all without any thought or conscious effort from yourself. Your body was designed to keep you balanced and healthy, and when you are out of alignment, your body will let you know. If you eat something that doesn't agree with your body, it'll show, sometimes in subtle ways, and other times, in more obvious ways. If you pay attention to your body after you eat, you may notice that perhaps certain foods cause you to feel bloated, gassy, or nauseous. You may experience sensations like pain and headaches. You may develop a rash or patches of dry, itchy skin.

Your body also communicates by showing external indicators of how well your internal systems are functioning through visible body parts like your skin, hair, nails, teeth, eyes, and tongue. When you're stressed, your body may hold tension, perhaps in your neck and shoulders, or you may feel knots in your stomach, or experience headaches. Whether it's obvious or subtle, you have the ability to learn how to tune into your body and recognize the signals it's sending. Your body is always communicating, you just have to know how to listen and understand the language it's speaking.

When your autonomic nervous system is working well, your body deals with negative stress by triggering the sympathetic nervous system and releasing chemicals that temporarily improve your performance. Cortisol, adrenaline, and other stress hormones increase heart rate, slow digestion, and increase blood pressure, all to allow greater blood flow to your muscles, heart, and brain so you can think or act quickly in the face of immediate or acute stress. It can give you a surge of adrenaline when you need energy to fight or escape a dangerous situation. There have been numerous cases of people performing miraculous feats of strength and/or endurance when dealing with life-or-death experiences, like a mother lifting part of a car off her child pinned underneath[1], or a seven-year-old boy who swam one mile to get help for his family that had been carried away by the current.[2] Once the stressful situation is over, the parasympathetic nervous system takes over, signalling to the brain to stop producing the stress hormones, allowing your body to relax and recover from the event.

Your body is capable of so much more than you know, and is more intelligent than you may give it credit for. It is this intelligence that you can tap into to help guide you to your best answers. When the answers are right for you, you may feel calmer, lighter, and more expansive. When the answers aren't right for you, you may feel agitated, heavier, or more closed off.

Listening to Your Body

In a well-known study called the Iowa Gambling Task[3], a team of neurologists and researchers from the University of Iowa designed a series of experiments to simulate real-life decision-making. They presented individual participants with four decks of cards with the given objective of winning as much play money as they could from turning over any of the cards from the decks, in any order they wished. The decks consisted of cards that indicated whether play money would be rewarded to them, or taken from them. What participants did not know was that two of the card decks were stacked to give net gains, while the other two would result in a net loss. Each participant was connected to a machine that measured the electrodermal activity of their skin, which detected a type of micro-sweating that indicated unconscious emotions. After participants (with normal cognitive functioning) turned over about ten cards, their palms started showing signs of micro-sweating when they reached for cards from the decks rigged with a net loss; however, it took them about another forty cards before they actually stopped picking cards from the net loss card decks, and could articulate that those decks were rigged. Their bodies were emitting signals through micro-sweating very early on in the experiment when they reached for the "bad" decks and made a detrimental decision, well before they were consciously aware and able to ascertain that the decks were rigged.

Many subsequent research studies have found that people who were more attuned to their bodies and gut instincts were better at decision-making, especially in stressful situations. Leveraging the findings from the Iowa Gambling Task study, a team from the University of Cambridge wanted to see if these findings extended to real-life decision-making. They examined successful financial traders and compared them against a control group matched for age and gender. Using two established heartbeat detection tasks, they asked each individual to tune into their heartbeats and measured the abilities of each person to accurately track their resting heartbeat. They found that the financial traders were significantly more attuned to their bodies and more adept at tracking their heartbeat compared to the general population (represented by the control group).[4]

Taking the study even further, they used data from the traders' financial performance, including portfolio profit and loss, and found that the more attuned a financial trader was to their body (via heartbeat detection), the more profitable and successful they were in risky decision-making. Within their line of work, these traders routinely made split-second financial decisions that could net or lose millions of dollars before being able to articulate the logical reasons behind the decisions. Recall that in the Iowa Gambling Task, participants' palms started to micro-sweat when reaching for the "bad" cards, which, in theory, could have helped steer them into better decision-making long before being consciously aware of the rigged decks—only if they were able to detect these bodily signals. Similarly, the University of Cambridge study found that the most profitable financial traders were the ones who were most attuned to their bodily signals to make split-second decisions using gut instincts.

The study also found that in general, financial traders were significantly more attuned to their bodies than the general population, in theory, because they were consciously or unconsciously leveraging the signals their bodies were sharing when making routine significant financial decisions in their jobs. Furthermore, researchers found a correlation between a trader's heartbeat detection abilities and how many years they survived as a successful trader in this cutthroat profession. The better they were at accurate heartbeat detection, the longer they lasted in the profession. This study reinforced previous findings of other research, positing that there is "evidence concerning the role of somatic signals, in other words, the body, in guiding our decision-making and behaviour and, crucially, our risk taking."

Your intelligent body is always communicating to help you make the best decisions, and those that are more adept at tuning into these signals have been proven to make more successful decisions. The good news is that you all have the ability to become more attuned to your bodies, and in turn, your gut instincts and intuition. You can improve your intuition skills by tuning into the signals your intelligent body is sending you. Meditation, mindfulness (discussed in Chapter 3), and the exercises outlined here can help you develop these abilities. Connecting deeper with my body was pivotal in my healing and growth, and this chapter is full of exercises for you to do The Work that will help you connect deeper, as well.

The Work – Heart Centered

You don't have to become a financial trader to improve your gut instincts. Let's start with a heartbeat meditation to help you turn your attention inwards, and become more aligned with your body. Please do not judge or criticize your experiences, thoughts, or feelings in meditation. Whatever you experience is perfectly fine.

Heartbeat Meditation

- Get into a comfortable meditation position. Sit, stand, or lie down with an open chest, relaxed, yet maintain a long neck and spine.
- Close your eyes or look downwards toward your nose in a soft gaze.
- Relax your body. Then, allow it to relax even more.
- Take a couple of deep breaths, in and out of your nose. Then, start to slow your breathing.
- Now, bring your awareness to your heart center, the space in the middle of your chest, behind your sternum/breastbone, in front of your spine.
- Notice how your breath moves in and out of your heart center. Keep your awareness on the sensations in your heart center.
- Once you've focused your awareness on your heart center for a while, see if you can notice your heartbeat.
- Keep your focus on your heartbeat for a few minutes, or on your heart center if you cannot yet feel your heartbeat.
- Bring your awareness back to your breath.
- Slowly open your eyes, and come out of the meditation when you feel ready.

Cultivating a regular meditation practice can help you become more attuned to your body and intuition. Chapter 3 will delve deeper into this topic.

Emotions

As you start doing The Work outlined in this book, many different emotions may start to surface. You may have noticed tightness or tension in the heartbeat meditation exercise, or perhaps it was very difficult for you to focus. Maybe it was hard to feel anything at all. Whatever your experience was, I assure you it is perfectly normal. You may be questioning your experience, thinking things like, *I'm not doing this right. I'm not good at this. I shouldn't feel this way.* But I urge you to do your best to recognize when you are judging or criticizing yourself, and then to stop and let it go. The Inner Work in Chapter 5 delves deeper into this topic, but for now, know that judgement and criticism of your efforts and experiences does not support you in any way. Let it all go.

Whatever emotions surface as you dive into The Work, know that your emotions are meant to be felt. Let yourself be with them, feel them, and allow them to pass. Your emotions are meant to move through you by experiencing them. If you try to deny or suppress them, they can weigh you down like an anchor. Judging your emotions simply adds more weight to them. They are not meant to be judged, just felt or acknowledged. Your feelings are your feelings. They are all energy. And they are not right or wrong. Acknowledge them—all of them, the good, bad, and ugly—and allow them to pass.

This doesn't mean you should take your feelings out on others when you're feeling angry or low, but instead, let yourself sit with them, recognize them, and ultimately allow them to pass. Cry, laugh, move, scream, or do what feels right, for this too shall pass. If you feel that you're overwhelmed by emotions from past traumas that are constantly replaying over and over again with no reprieve, it may be helpful to speak with others or a professional that can help you move through those emotions as they hold space for you.

Tapping into Our Intuition for Our Best Answers

Something that has worked well for me is tuning into my body, connecting to my body's intelligence, and asking questions. One of the first times I tried this, I was surprised to find that my head was nodding *yes* or shaking side to side for *no*. I was expecting to feel the more subtle signs of openness or tightness (which I had previously experienced), or to feel a yes/no inside of myself, but I got very obvious answers with my head nodding or shaking. I doubted my answers, feeling unsure about where they came from, so, I made sure to ground myself, connect with my body, higher self, and those here for my highest and greatest good. I asked for my ego to step aside. And over time, it became easier to trust the answers. Sometimes, the answers came back as feelings—often even before I finished asking my question internally. When I tried The Work exercise below with food, I very clearly got the message to stop eating bread (including the organic, sprouted, whole grain, gluten-free bread that I ate, and my husband and daughter said tasted like cardboard). My body corroborated that I should stop eating dairy, which I had already gathered from the signs it gave me in my skin and body over the years. I also understood that I should stop eating eggs, which I loved. When my body underwent changes, I asked and got answers to explain why, like why my period came earlier (because I had started taking supplements that were helping cleanse my body). I also got the message several times to drink lots of water, to help detox as my body experiences changes.

When you are open to answers, feeling balanced and good, your gut and body will give you answers that best match your state. If you ask questions while feeling fearful and low, afraid of outcomes or consequences, understand that the answers may come from fear, meaning that the responses you receive may stem from your ego trying to protect you. Remember that there are no wrong decisions; however, making a decision in fear may lead to your ego stepping in front of your internal wisdom to steer you toward "safer" choices that may only perpetuate your state of fear because that is what you know, and that is what you're used to. If you're reading this book, I know that you don't want to continue living in fear, so, do your best to approach your questions from a place of peace, alignment, and balance. Your body will speak to you, aligning with your energy and spirit. As you go through The Work exercises outlined below, do your best to feel relaxed, connected, and calm before starting, so you can receive the best answers for yourself. If you're going in feeling like it won't work, fearful of the answers you may receive, or experiencing some other stressed or fearful reaction, the answers that come may reflect that fear. Do your best to remain open, relaxed, and calm.

The Work – Feeling Your Food

Many of us have foods that may not agree well with us when eaten. For example, when I eat dairy, my stomach will get bloated and gassy. But when I was growing up, I wasn't aware of the fact that my body was trying to tell me something about the food I was consuming daily. To me, it was normal to experience bloating and gas because it had always been that way. I didn't realize that I didn't have to feel like that all the time. It wasn't until I started paying closer attention to my diet and the way my body felt after I ate that I noticed certain foods had different effects on me. Too much processed, white food left me tired, while dairy left me bloated and constipated. After my daughter was born, I developed mild rosacea on my cheeks and noticed that it flared up when I consumed dairy or gluten and was minimized when I avoided these foods.

If you're trying to eat healthier and start doing research on the topic, it may become overwhelming, as there is a wealth of information out there, and the advice can be confusing or even conflicting at times. *Eat whole grains, don't eat any grains. Eat pastured meat, don't eat any meat. Drink coffee, don't drink coffee.* The fact is, one diet does not fit all, since we are all living in different environments, at different life stages, and dealing with different ailments or conditions. So, what can you do? Educate yourself, learn from the experts, read the research, consult medical professionals, and tune into your gut and body to feel the best answer for *you*. Your body will know what's best for you at that time. And keep tuning in because the answers may change over time as your health and environment shifts.

When you become more attuned to your body, you can better gauge whether certain foods will agree with you or not. Here's an exercise to help evaluate which foods may be best for you by tapping into your body's wisdom:

- Take a few slow deep breaths, allowing your body to relax.
- Bring your awareness to your solar plexus (your gut, the space above the belly button and below the chest), and the space in the center of your chest, the heart center. Notice the sensations in these areas and soften this space.
- Next, shift your awareness to the food you wish to evaluate by looking at it, thinking about it, saying the name internally or aloud, or holding it, and then notice how your body reacts.
- Notice if your solar plexus or heart center feels open and relaxed, or if it tightens up and feels closed off. If your body responds by feeling open, relaxed, and expansive, that means that particular food may be right for you. Conversely, if your body tightens up, jerks, or feels closed off, then that particular food may not be best for you.
- You may need to try this exercise several times to practice and understand the difference between feeling open and expansive, versus feeling tight and restricted. Try not to get frustrated if it doesn't come easily at first.

Try this exercise with some of your favourite foods, foods that you feel may not agree with you, and foods that you think are healthy.

Your Body's Connection to the Earth

How you treat your body is inextricably linked to how you treat the earth. Our bodies are deeply connected to the earth and vice versa. We were conceived on this earth, are nourished and sustained by this earth, and when we die, our bodies return to the earth. From a simply material perspective, you can see that the choices we make for our bodies in the food that we buy and eat affects the way we treat the planet. Mindfully eating more whole and organic foods is not only healthier for our bodies, but also for the earth and its inhabitants. Consider the following as an example:

- Eating less processed foods = less pollution, less destruction of resources on the earth
- Binging on more food than we need = overloading our bodies = depleting the earth by taking more than we need
- Eating organic = treating the earth better with fewer pesticides, increasing ecology and soil health

When you are treating your body with respect and taking care of its health, you, in turn, will be showing more respect to Mother Earth, and taking better care of her health and that of all beings.

The Work – Feeling Your Answers

Think of a time when you were feeling happy, calm, and safe. How did your body feel? It's likely that your body was relaxed and open. Conversely, in situations where you are stressed or feeling insecure, your body will respond with an elevated heart rate, tightened muscles, quickened breath, and higher blood pressure.

Start becoming more attuned to your body and how it feels. Notice when you're feeling tightness in the chest or feeling light and free. Sayings like "I felt it in my gut", or "I had a sinking feeling in my stomach" are common because they are true. Your gut instincts are your body's way of communicating with you. Recognize how your body feels and what's happening in the situation the next time something like this happens, and make a mental note of it. These cues are sending you messages and you can learn how to read them.

For this exercise, you may need to try it several times to practice and understand the difference in feeling open and expansive, versus feeling tight and restricted. It is helpful to practice beforehand to help distinguish the feelings by posing a question and evaluating options where you already clearly know the truth or the best answers for you. Practice bringing in answers that you know are right or wrong, and see how that feels.

- Think about any question that you're looking to get the best answer to. You may want to write it down.
- Consider and outline all the options for your answer, clearly articulating them in your mind, and/or write each option down.
- Now, take a few deep breaths and start relaxing your body. Tune into your body and feel yourself in your

body, feel the energy inside your body, and feel the energy all around it.

- Ask your body for internal wisdom (or whatever you want to call it) to help guide you to the best answer for you. You may wish to politely ask your ego to step aside.

- Once you feel calm, connect to the space in your heart center and consider your question. Bring that question into your heart center if that makes sense for you.

- Let the question go, and bring forward one answer or option to the question. Hold this answer in your heart center and try to feel it in your body. Imagine you have chosen this answer. How does this feel in your body? Visualize what the answer could look like if that makes sense. Notice how your gut, chest, and shoulders feel. Do they feel open and light, or tight and constricted? What do you notice or experience? Note and write down how your body responded to that option.

- Let that option go, breathe, and feel your body again.

- Now, bring in the next option, holding it in your heart center. Again, notice how it feels in your body. Does your body feel light, relaxed, or expansive? Notice how your gut, chest, and shoulders feel. Does your body feel tight, constricted, or closed off? What do you notice or experience? Note and write down how your body responded to that option.

- Continue this exercise for each of the options you have for the question you posed.

- When you have finished, take some time to consider how your body reacted to each answer. Did any of the answers intuitively feel best for you? Notice which answers your body felt the most relaxed, open, and expansive in. Were there any that elicited tightness or tension? The answer where you felt the most open and expansive is the one that is best for you.

Connect with Your Body

Deepening the connection with your body enables you to better tune into your own inner wisdom. This inner wisdom can help quietly guide you when faced with a difficult question or situation. Your inner wisdom knows what's best for you, and if you can learn to tune in, you can feel it, hear it, and understand it. You can get there with practice because you've undoubtedly tuned into your intuition before.

I've outlined how our bodies are intelligent and always communicating with us. However, everyone's relationship with their body is different, and many of you may have grown up feeling ashamed or resentful of your bodies. Even now, as adults, many of you may feel that your body isn't enough—be it thin enough, curvy enough, strong enough, good enough—whatever the limiting belief is about your body that you have ingrained. Your body feels this fear, pain, and loathing. Yet, it is here for you, to serve you, to help you get through every day on earth. Helping you live, breathe, move, and feel. When you can learn to accept, forgive, and love your body and yourself unconditionally, a deeper connection forms. You become more attuned to your body—more whole. This brings with it several benefits, including becoming more connected to your body's intelligence and your inner wisdom. It makes it easier to notice when something isn't right for you by the way your body feels, reacts, tenses, or closes. You're able to become more aware of when something is right for you, as your body will feel more relaxed, open, light, and expansive.

The connection to your body enables access to a greater intelligence and inner wisdom. From my experience, I've come to realize that accessing our intuition and wisdom becomes easier when we fully accept and love our whole selves, which includes our bodies. Once I understood this connection, I also realized that at some point in my life, I was critical of almost every part of my body—my feet were too wide, my nails weren't right, I had cellulite on my legs, bumps on my skin, and so on. I have no doubt that many of you have done the same to your own bodies, and you can work through this, just as I did. Once I recognized how critical I had been, I actively worked to love, praise, and respect each part of my body, working from my toes to the top of my head, thanking the muscles, organs, tissues, bones, nerves, and all the cells for all that they've done to help keep me healthy and moving. And I repeated this exercise many times, as I knew there was a lifetime of judgement and criticism, so, it would inevitably take time to undo that and fill my body with love instead.

The Work – Loving our Bodies

As I've progressed in my journey, healed, and balanced my body, I came to recognize that while my body has been here to serve me in many ways, I have been very critical of it for most of my life. So, to help heal, balance, and connect more deeply, I started connecting with and feeling each part of my body in meditation, expressing my love and gratitude, and blessing it for the highest and greatest good.

Body Scan & Gratitude Meditation

- Get into a comfortable meditation position. Sit, stand, or lie down with an open chest, relaxed, yet maintain a long neck and spine.
- Close your eyes if that feels comfortable, or look downwards toward your nose in a soft gaze. Relax your body.
- Take a few deep breaths, in and out of your nose, slowing your breathing. Relax your body even more.
- Start your body scan at the soles of your feet, then work your way up toward your head, taking time to focus on one part of your body at a time.
- For each part of your body you're focusing on, notice any sensations or feelings in that area, and try to let go of any tension.
- Thank each part of your body as you are focused on it, send it love and gratitude, and bless it for your greatest good.
- Focus on each area of your body for a while before letting go and gently moving up to the next.
- Slowly work through each part of your body, starting at your feet and ending at the top of your head. You may

wish to reverse the order, and/or work your way up and down your body.

- When you're finished with the body scan, turn your awareness into the space and energy inside your whole body for a few moments. Simply notice any feelings or experiences without any judgement.
- Bring your awareness back to your breathing.
- Slowly open your eyes.

I encourage you to also try this exercise in front of a mirror, to help connect more with each part of your body as you feel appreciation for it. However you approach it and whatever your experience is, know that it is perfectly fine. The goal of this exercise is to simply connect to our body and send it gratitude and love.

The Intuitive Body

Over the years, as my yoga and meditation practices deepened, they evolved to become one intuitive practice. A few years ago, after a very intense meditation, I felt my body being moved by energy outside of my physical body, which was very shocking and surprising. It moved me into a yoga practice with asanas, stretches, and breathing. As I allowed the energy to move my body, I was still in disbelief. Now I know that the energy was not outside of me, but within me—it was me. I am the energy. I am connected and attuned to the energy to a point where my movements are not predetermined by my mind; my mind is not controlling my body. My body moves in a way that is best for me, putting me in positions and poses that loosen areas that are tight and strengthens those I don't realize are weak. Since that moment, I've continued with my intuitive practice and have been able to continuously balance my body, which was more out of balance than I even realized. My whole right side had been tight and restricted for so long, governed and overworked by the dominance of masculine yang energies in my life, like logic, achieving, and thinking. I finally allowed that side to rest more and come back into balance with the feminine yin side. My feminine yin energies started to become more engaged, strengthened, and balanced, as did my body, brain, and the corresponding muscles and tissues.

As I became more connected and attuned to my body, I realized that I'd always had injuries on the right side of my body. I had sprained my right ankle multiple times, hurt my right shoulder doing a shoulder press during my CrossFit years, and had carpal tunnel in my right arm. Once I started re-balancing my body, different areas started to release that I didn't even realize were tight or seized. I noticed one day that my hips felt different as I walked, that I could feel the now fluid movement in my hip socket that I didn't even notice was tight for years.

As I became more connected with my energy, my awareness expanded. I started to recognize and notice constrictions I felt on my right side. During meditations and body scans, I realized it was harder to feel the energy and sensations on certain areas on my right side, like around my torso or the top of my head. I remembered that when I breastfed my daughter and pumped, most of the milk came from my left breast, as my right breast produced milk very slowly. I noticed when breathing mindfully and deeply, it was more difficult to fill up my right lung and that it didn't feel as full as breathing into my left lung. With time and daily practice, I slowly noticed changes, as I allowed energy to move my body to where it needed to be. I started opening up, gaining strength, and balancing myself. Seeing an osteopath helped with opening up my right side. My right ankle gained more flexion and range of motion. Massage therapy and TCM (Traditional Chinese Medicine) cupping appointments helped me further release any tension I was housing.

A couple of years after I became more connected with my body and allowed it to move intuitively, I noticed a profound difference. One day, I was leading a guided meditation class and suddenly felt profoundly expanded and light. In this lightness, I felt balanced and open, and I realized the feeling was because my right side had opened up expansively, and that the energy was moving more freely. It's felt amazing because I didn't even know I could feel that way—that light and open. When you become attuned to your body and your energy, and allow them to regain balance with your mind, you open yourself up to new possibilities, feelings, and answers.

CHAPTER 3

Making Space for Your Answers with Meditation

In the nothing, there is everything.

THE DAY I received the cancer diagnosis, I had dinner with my cousins. It was planned before I knew what was going to happen, and despite being in shock from the diagnosis, I decided not to cancel. When I shared with them what had happened earlier that day, there were tears, hugs, words of encouragement and consolation. While chatting with one of my cousins, she told me about a book that she felt may be helpful, *Becoming Supernatural* by Joe Dispenza. I was open to anything, so, I promptly ordered it. The book shared tools and meditation practices to shift your mindset and recondition your body to change your reality, including your health, and scientific research to support the transformations. I had prior experience with meditation through my yoga training and practice, a Mindfulness-Based Stress Reduction course I'd taken years earlier, as well as a couple of retreats and classes. As a child, I also frequented Buddhist temples with my grandmother, and participated with the monks in their meditation practice. One of the earliest home videos I saw of myself was of me meditating in a lotus position as my siblings tried to distract me. Despite all this exposure and experience, I had not maintained a consistent, daily meditation practice. Instead, I generally practiced meditation weekly, and used it as a coping tool for when I became anxious or stressed to help me calm down.

This changed after my diagnosis when I decided to cultivate a daily meditation practice. While I already had a feeling—a knowing sense that everything would be fine before I started meditating daily—the practice helped me connect back to that knowing whenever fears and doubts crept in. Early on, when I was just starting my daily practice, I sat on the couch, reading the instructions for a body chakra meditation, and then put the book down to try the meditation myself. Soon, my upper body began to sway in circles. I wasn't sure what was happening, and the swaying lasted a couple of hours, even as I sat on the couch googling, "Why am I swaying in circles during meditation?" I knew right then that I had tapped into something deeper, and felt encouraged to keep meditating daily.

Over the years, my meditation practice has evolved. I didn't confine myself to the belief that there was only one path or type of meditation that was best, and simply practiced the ones that resonated with me at that time. As I was grappling with the diagnosis, I was drawn to Metta, the loving-kindness practice, because the mantras and words rang true to me and were easy to focus on. Whenever I was in the hospital for any appointment or procedure, I was always meditating in the waiting room.

Before my surgery, instead of sitting in the waiting room with the rest of the patients and their loved ones, I paced the halls in a walking loving-kindness meditation in my hospital gown and socks. The practice helped ground me, and helped keep me calmer, present, and grateful in a difficult situation. In the operating room, the last thing I remember before going under was expressing my gratitude out loud to the doctors, nurses, and staff in the room as I shed silent tears. My meditation practice enabled me to be more present, resilient, and healthy during and after my cancer journey.

Making Space for your Answers

Like many of you, my mind used to race with thoughts and worries, playing an ongoing commentary in the background. It was harder to hear the best answers for myself when there was no space between my thoughts, as they piled up against one another. Many of those thoughts were worries and concerns of what could happen in the future, along with regret, judgement, and criticism of the past over what I'd done or not done. I know many of you can relate and easily recall times in your life when anxiety took over; you're not alone. Feelings of anxiety have only increased in recent years. In fact, 62% of respondents to a 2020 survey indicated they had experienced some degree of anxiety.[5] The Anxiety and Depression Association of America reported that almost one-third (31%) of adults will experience an anxiety disorder at some point in their life,[6] and that number increased during the COVID-19 pandemic, with

41.5% of adults reporting symptoms of anxiety or depressive disorders.[7] What is important to note, however, is that the vast majority of things people worry about never occur, and if they do, they are able to handle it better than anticipated. A study named *Exposing Worry's Deceit* found that 91.4% of worries that people with generalized anxiety disorder (GAD) had did not come true. (GAD is the most common anxiety disorder, which is described as persistent, excessive, and uncontrollable anxiety and worry about everyday life events.)[8] Moreover, research indicates that when the outcome was negative, participants coped with those outcomes better than feared 79% of the time.[9] This means that the overwhelming majority of worries and anxieties people have don't come true, and if they do, they are better able to cope with them than they expect, and can even learn from the experience. People are more resilient than they believe. You are more resilient than you believe.

All the worries and ruminations taking up space in your mind aren't necessary, and only cause more anxiety and stress. When you start quieting your mind and opening more space between your thoughts, it clears the way for your best answers to come through. Meditation helps to access that empty space between your thoughts, where you are connected to your inner self and all that is around you. This is where your best answers and inspiration can be found more easily. However, with all the noise and ongoing chatter in our minds, it can make it harder to hear and feel our own wisdom and intuition. This is where meditation and mindfulness are so helpful.

I have received several inspired thoughts just when being present and mindful in everyday tasks, like brushing my teeth.

Being present means that I am where I am, with all my senses. I am not in the past reliving an experience, nor thinking or worrying about a future "what-if" scenario. I am simply present with my mind, body, and soul. I can be simply brushing my teeth when an idea or thought suddenly pops into my mind. It feels random, but it isn't. It is a message—a connection or energy that managed to surface when I was more present and connected to my inner self. You've had this before when someone comes to mind and then you hear or see them soon after. When I started getting deeper in my meditation practice and connecting more with my inner wisdom, I noticed a pattern. As various people in my life began to pop up in my mind, I noticed after connecting with them that whenever they had seemingly "randomly" come to my attention, they were going through a difficult time in their lives, dealing with depression, illness, family deaths, or marital discord. I learned to reach out to people when they came up in my mind, just to let them know I was there and thinking of them, and available if they wanted to talk. It was what I felt I was supposed to do.

What is Meditation? What is Mindfulness?

You may have tried meditation or mindfulness before, or even taken a class or two. Some of you may even practice meditation on your own. There is a reason why it is growing and resonating with so many people. But what is meditation or mindfulness? It is focusing, reflecting, contemplating, and being. Jon Kabat-Zinn, a meditation teacher renowned for helping to integrate mindfulness into Western medicine and society, has defined mindfulness meditation as "the awareness that arises from paying attention, on purpose, in the present moment and non-judgmentally."[10] Meditation is simply being present and tuned in, with your awareness open and attention focused, and with no judgement. You may find many different definitions of meditation and mindfulness; however, it is simply being present, here, aware in the now, and connected to your senses. A simple delineation of the definitions I resonate with is that mindfulness is focusing on *some*-thing (like a candle, picture, washing the dishes, eating, and so on), whereas meditation is focusing on *no*-thing (something intangible, like space or feelings). It is tuning into yourself, what's around you, and your object of focus. And an important part of the practice is no judgment or criticism of the experience or yourself.

Meditation helps you connect with yourself, your energy, your body, and your mind. It helps you feel more, and also sense blocks and imbalances. It helps you shift the focus away from the internal chatter that's telling you what you should do, fixates on what went wrong or could go wrong, and wallows in self-pity and fear. It helps you understand that you are not your thoughts; instead, you are the observer of your thoughts. It helps you realize that you are not the running commentary in your mind, nor are you defined by it. It helps you connect with your inner self, feel more trusting and confident in yourself, and even in the unknown to come.

Benefits of Meditation

Science is just scratching the surface on what meditation can do. There are thousands of studies out there showing the benefits of a meditation or mindfulness practice. Some of these include:[11]

- Improve well-being
- Reduce stress
- Reduce anxiety and anxiety-related mental health issues like social anxiety, phobias, and obsessive-compulsive behaviours
- Mitigate depression
- Improve self-awareness
- Increase attention span
- Improve memory and mental clarity
- Increase compassion and empathy
- Improve willpower and mental discipline
- Improve sleep quality
- Diminish perception of pain
- Lower blood pressure

Meditation *literally* changes your brain. Scientists used to believe that human brains were static after development into adulthood, meaning that they did not change or grow. However, we know now that our nervous system and brain are malleable, plastic—The least used neural connections are pruned, while the ones we use and exercise are strengthened.[12] For example, if you start to learn how to juggle, the areas of the brain responsible for visuals and hand eye coordination will have increased activity and more neural connections will be formed. Conversely, when you stop using and practicing things you've learned, like a language or a musical instrument you played growing up, neural connections associated with that activity will be pruned, and your ability to engage in those activities diminishes.

So, what happens when you meditate? The benefits and results will differ depending on the type of meditation practiced, as well as the duration; however, studies have shown that brain matter increases in the areas of the brain activated during meditation, leading to improved processing and abilities. Thus, when you are consciously engaging your brain in a meditation where you are aware, focused, and present, the areas of the brain associated with self-awareness, attention, and being in the present moment are activated, and more neural connections are formed in those regions, which increases grey matter.

There are many different types of meditation, but they all generally involve relaxing, tuning inward, and focusing on your chosen object of attention. Research has shown that different types of meditation have various effects on human brains and behaviour. For example, loving-kindness meditation, which includes feeling and sending loving thoughts to yourself and others, increases feelings of compassion and empathy for others more than other meditation practices. Mindfulness meditation with a focused attention on a particular thing or object improves attention and concentration.

It's been shown that as we age, grey matter in our brain decreases, which is associated with decreased memory and cognitive processing abilities. MRI images of meditators have shown increased grey matter in the prefrontal cortex and the areas of the brain responsible for decision-making, memory, as well as sensory, cognitive and emotional processing.[13] In one study, MRI images of meditators compared with non-meditators showed that 50-year-old meditators had the same amount of cortex and grey matter as 25-year-old non-meditators.[14] In other studies, MRI images of non-meditators before and after taking an eight-week Mindfulness-Based Stress Reduction (MBSR) course showed increased density in grey matter concentration of brain regions involved in learning and memory processes, emotion regulation, empathy and compassion, and perspective taking.[15]

Conversely, studies have shown that the amygdala, the area of the brain that regulates the "fight, flight or freeze" stress response (also known as the fight, flight, freeze or fawn response), decreases in volume with meditation, which is correlated with an increased ability to deal with stress and anxiety.[16] The amygdala is a primal region of the brain, associated with fear and emotion, as well as the driver of the body's response to stress. When you are put into a sustained stressful situation, your amygdala increases, putting you in a fight, flight or freeze mode with elevated stress hormones coursing through you, even if there is no imminent threat outside of the fear in your mind. For many of you, your stress and fears are created from ruminating over negative "what if" scenarios that may never occur, or past difficult situations that are on replay in your mind. These fears, ruminations, and worries of the future and past produce a very real impact on your mind and body. Meditation can help by reducing the amygdala's volume, which enables you to better cope with stress and anxiety.[17]

Meditation and Your Body

In a stressful situation, your body's autonomic nervous system will respond by activating the sympathetic nervous system to trigger the fight, flight or freeze response and deal with the stress, and then the parasympathetic nervous system ("rest and digest") to help you recover from that stress once the situation is over.[18] When your autonomic nervous system is working well, your body deals with negative stress by triggering the sympathetic nervous system and releasing chemicals that temporarily improve your performance. Cortisol, adrenaline, and other stress hormones increase heart rate, slow digestion, and increase blood pressure, all to allow greater blood flow to your muscles, heart, and brain to be able to think or act quickly in the face of immediate or acute stress. Acting together, stress hormones ensure that you can think and act quickly and clearly in stressful situations. In addition to creating the emergency response, stress hormones divert energy away from non-emergency functions like digestion, reproduction, and maintaining the immune system. When the stressful situation is over, your body is able to recover from this acute stress via a natural feedback loop with the brain. High levels of stress hormones in the blood signal to the brain to stop producing the stress hormones so you can rest and recover from the stressful event.

With acute stress, once the perceived threat has passed, the parasympathetic nervous system takes over, allowing you to relax and recover from the stressful event. Chronic stress is ongoing stress that seems endless, such as a demanding job, difficult family life, or experiencing ongoing hardship. Chronic stress, severe trauma, and post-traumatic stress disorder (PTSD) can be very damaging when your autonomic nervous system's natural feedback loop becomes interrupted, thus not giving your body a chance to recover as it is continually exposed to the hormones that regulate stress. Chronic stress, severe trauma, and PTSD can interrupt the pattern of the nervous system turning on to help rest and digest after the fight, flight or freeze response. The relaxation response is not activated, and the pathway that regulates cortisol is shut down, rendering it unable to stop the effects of the stress. It is the constant activation of the stress response that can lead to many health issues seen with chronic stress, severe trauma, and PTSD.

Meditation has been shown to help better regulate your autonomic nervous system and turn on your parasympathetic nervous system to allow your body to take care of itself and heal as it was designed to do. Many studies have shown the benefits of a meditation practice include the ability to feel calmer and more relaxed. This is because when you meditate, you activate the parasympathetic nervous system (rest and digest response), the part of your autonomic nervous system responsible for helping you recover from stress.

It is important to note, however, that if you are dealing with chronic stress, PTSD, or have experienced severe trauma, while meditation has many proven benefits, it may feel even more challenging for you to establish a meditation practice on your own. This is because your body and nervous system haven't been able to fully activate the parasympathetic nervous system (rest and digest response) to process and integrate the fight, flight or freeze response to the chronic stress or severe trauma. Once you start engaging in a meditation practice that activates the parasympathetic nervous system (rest and digest), you are allowing your body to integrate the stress, and that discharged energy moving through you may re-trigger traumatic experiences or memories. This is normal and will feel different for everyone. You may start suddenly crying, shaking, sweating, or experiencing other physical reactions. Think of a deer that freezes and plays dead when unable to escape from a perceived hunter. When the deer gets a chance to escape, it will shake its body to discharge and integrate the stress. Some people can manage this on their own, discharge the energy and integrate the trauma, thus allowing it to pass, but for others, it may be more difficult, and can potentially put them back into a loop of replaying trauma without integration. In these cases, I highly suggest working with a professional to help you integrate the trauma and stress in a way that feels safe for you. *Trauma-Sensitive Mindfulness* by David A. Treleaven is also a great resource for those who have experienced severe trauma and are looking to learn more about establishing a meditation practice.

No matter what your past experiences are, I want everyone to understand that you are in control of your meditation practice. You decide where and when to meditate, how to position yourself, whether to have your eyes open or closed, what your attention is focused on, when to move, and when to stop. Do not try to force a meditation. Do not assume there is only one way to meditate properly. Listen to yourself and listen to your body. Take your time, and do what feels right for you. No one else can tell you what that is.

No Expectations, No Judgements

As a teacher of meditation, I have learned that many people feel they cannot meditate or do it properly because their minds are busy, constantly drifting away to other thoughts or distractions instead of being present in the moment. This is not true; anyone can meditate. I always tell people not to worry or put themselves down if their mind wanders because that is natural. Noticing when your mind has wandered, and then gently guiding it back to your object of attention without any judgement or criticism is a big part of meditation. That act of being aware that your mind has wandered, acknowledging it, and coming back is part of your meditation practice. There is nothing wrong with that, and you are strengthening your practice every time you do that. Once that happens, let go of the distraction, and come back to your focus with no judgement. The more you do that, over and over again, the easier it gets, and the longer you will go between distractions or thoughts taking your attention off your focus of meditation.

What *is* important is to do your best not to have any expectations, and not to judge or criticize your experience or practice. Judging or criticizing your experience or thoughts does not help you. When you become aware that your mind has wandered, that you're thinking of something else, let it go and come back to your meditation practice. Don't fixate on what you feel isn't going well, as that won't lead to a solution. Do your best to not judge yourself or your thoughts. Instead, treat yourself with empathy and kindness because that is part of your practice. Treating yourself with empathy and kindness is self-love and healing, and can help you transform and shift, little by little. One day at a time. One meditation practice at a time.

How Do You Meditate and Be Mindful?

Whether you've realized it or not, you've already done this before. Maybe while you were driving, cooking, cleaning, singing, dancing, doing yoga, walking, or running. It is any time you've been "in the zone", focused, and at ease. It is not about stopping your thoughts or not thinking, but rather it is about focusing on something—be it your breath, an image, mantra, a body part, feelings, and so on—and allowing your mind to relax in awareness. You can be mindful in every present moment of your life. It is being in the now—the present moment—instead of thinking about the future or the past.

- Instead of waking up and immediately checking your phone, thinking about what you're doing next, or what's going to happen in your day, just be present in bed.
- Instead of brushing your teeth and thinking about breakfast, what you're going to wear, the work you need to do, or the lunch you have to make, just be present while you brush your teeth.
- Instead of commuting and thinking about your to-do list, the meetings you have, or checking your phone, just be present while you walk, drive, bike, or take transit.
- Instead of worrying about what you did wrong in the past, mistakes, what you shouldn't have said, shouldn't

have done, or shouldn't have eaten, just be present where you are.

Be Aware of the Ego

At first, as you tune in to try and connect to your best answers, it may be easy to get confused by the answers your ego gives you, sometimes referred to as the judge or inner critic. That is the voice running in your mind that tells you what you should've done or what's likely going to go wrong. That ego voice is fearful of the unknown and wants to protect you. It may be helpful at times for planning, or in life and death scenarios, but for most people, that ego voice takes over and dominates your headspace 24/7. I want you to know that the ego voice is not the inner wisdom you are seeking for your best answers. It may be confusing and tricky as you start to mindfully tune inward to connect to your inner wisdom because your ego voice has consistently reigned over your thoughts. I used to identify with that voice. I thought *I* was that voice. However, once I started practicing meditation, observing, and learning more, I recognized that it wasn't me speaking; it was my ego.

The ego is often the loudest voice in your head, and for most of my life, it dominated the conversation in my mind. Nowadays, my ego is fairly quiet; however, it didn't quietly fade away. As a mentor said to me when I grappled with the ego trying to assert control, "That ego bitch isn't happy that it's no longer in charge." There was a resistance as I started gaining awareness that I was not my ego, and I did not need to listen to the ego.

As you start to tune into your inner wisdom and self, pay attention to the answers and messages you receive to decipher if the answers you're receiving are from your ego or true inner self. To help delineate between the two, sit with your answers. Be with them. How do they feel to you? Do you feel any judgement? Is it an answer in reaction to fear, or is it trying to protect you from possible failure? If there is judgement or fear, that is an answer from the ego. I have learned to ground myself and be heart-centered before tuning inwards for answers, which helps ensure the answers I'm receiving are for my highest and greatest good, and from my true inner being.

Tuning into your heart and gut instincts to guide you in your life journey and choices will serve you best. As you start to hone your intuition, it may be helpful to ask your ego to kindly step aside when you tune in to connect with your inner self for wisdom and answers. The answers you listen to and the choices that you make need to *feel* right for you. Do what resonates with you. You are in charge; you are in control.

When I first started practicing meditation, I had read that meditation helps you connect with the space between your thoughts, and my first thought was, *What space?* My thoughts ran into and overlapped one another, leaving no room for anything else to come through. But once I was able to pay attention to them, observe, and become aware of the running ego commentary, I started understanding that I could take back control. I could stop the ego commentary and redirect my focus to something else, like my breath, body, or heart. Inevitably, the voice would start up again. *Oh, this is so hard. I'm always thinking—that's just how I've always been. I'm an analytical over-*

thinker. But I learned that it was okay to let go of that thought without judgement, re-focusing on my breath, body, heart, or mantra. I did this over and over and over and over again. Then, I did it some more. It got easier with time. When I first recognized there was even just a glimpse of space between my thoughts, I was amazed. *Wow, there really is space there.* As I practiced, that space got larger and larger. After a week-long meditation retreat, I was able to stay present for a whole day before my first thought that broke the silence was, *I haven't had a thought in a day.*

It is in this space where your best answers will come through. It is always accessible within you. You can do this.

The Work – Get Ready to Meditate

- Find a quiet space where you ideally won't be disturbed, and turn off or mute your phone. Not being disturbed is useful when you are cultivating your meditation practice, but don't be discouraged if it's difficult to find a space with peace and quiet as you can practice any-where, even with potential distractions.
- If you like, you can have calming music playing in the background, or none at all.
- You can practice meditation sitting in a chair, on the floor, or laying down (standing and walking are also options):
  - Sitting in a chair: Sit up straight yet comfortably. Keep both feet flat on the ground with your knees

bent around 90 degrees. Your hands can be in a comfortable position on your lap, palms up or down.

  ○ Sitting on the floor: As above, sit up straight, yet comfortably. If you're not used to sitting on the floor for long periods of time, you may want to sit on a meditation cushion, pillow, or folded towel. Placing it under your sit bones may help you be more comfortable, with your knees ideally lower than your hips. Try not to sit in a position that cuts off circulation to your lower limbs, so, you may wish to uncross your legs or ankles.

  ○ Laying down: Lie down comfortably with a straight neck and spine, relaxing your chest and body. If you keep falling asleep while meditating laying down, you may want to try a different position.

• Whatever position you are in, ensure you have an erect yet relaxed neck and spine. Relax your shoulders and chest.

• Ensure you are comfortable. If while in meditation you feel the urge to adjust your position from discomfort and are unable to focus on anything else, feel free to move mindfully, and then return your awareness to your meditation focus.

• Remember that you are in control, and at any point, you may come out of the meditation.

• Do your best not to judge your experience or thoughts, and to have no expectations.

Breath Meditation

- Get into a comfortable meditation position.
- Close your eyes (or look down toward your nose in a soft gaze) and relax your body.
- Inhale deeply, and slowly let go of the breath through your mouth with a *haaa* sound. Repeat a couple more times until you feel more relaxed.
- Come back to breathing in and out of your nose.
- Keep your awareness on your breath. Simply notice your breathing. Notice the sounds, the feeling of the breath, the breath as it moves in and out of your body.
- If a thought or distraction comes in, notice it, let go without judgment, and return your focus to your breath.
- Keep your focus on your breathing for at least five minutes (or what feels best for you).
- Bring your attention back to your body.
- Take your time and slowly open your eyes.
- Remember: Be kind to your thoughts, try not to judge or be uncomfortable with them.

Body Scan Meditation

- Get into a comfortable meditation position.
- Close your eyes and relax your body.
- Take a couple of deep breaths, in and out of your nose. Try to slow your breathing.

- Start your body scan, moving your awareness from the soles of your feet to the top of your head, focusing on one part of your body at a time. For each part of your body, notice any sensations you may or may not have there. Try to relax that space and breathe into it, if that makes sense to you. Soften it and let go. Then, move to the next body part and repeat. Scan through your body. This may take anywhere from 10 to 60+ minutes:
  - Soles of your feet, toes, tops, and backs of your feet. Both feet, inside and out.
  - Ankles
  - Lower legs (your calves and shins)
  - Knees
  - Upper legs (your thighs, hamstrings, and quads)
  - Pelvic floor, hips, and bum
  - Lower belly, just below your belly button
  - Solar plexus (space above your belly button and below your chest, around your rib cage)
  - Chest and heart center
  - Shoulders, arms, and hands
  - Upper back, mid-back, and lower back
  - Neck and throat
  - Jaw, mouth, and tongue
  - Eyelids, eyebrows, temples, and forehead
  - Sides and back of the head
  - Top of your head
- Turn your awareness back to your inner body.
- Bring your awareness back to breathing.
- When you feel ready, slowly open your eyes.

Heart Centered Meditation

- Get into a comfortable meditation position.
- Close your eyes and relax your body.
- Take a couple of deep breaths, in and out of your nose. Start to slow your breathing.
- Bring your awareness to your heart center. This is the space in the center of your chest, inside your body, behind the breastbone (sternum), and in front of your spine.
- Breathe in and out of your heart center, feeling the space and energy there. Notice any sensations or experiences you may have.
- If you notice any tension or tightness, simply do so without judgement. If you wish, you may try to let go of any tension you may be holding onto and soften this space.
- Keep your awareness in your heart center for at least five to ten minutes.
- Place your right hand on top of your chest, and your left hand on top of your right. Breathe deeply, feeling the space in your heart center, behind your palms.
- Bring your awareness back to your breath.
- Take your time and slowly open your eyes when you're ready.

Walking to Your Answers

Earlier, I mentioned being mindful in your daily activities, like when you wake up in the morning, brush your teeth, take a shower, and eat your meals. Another everyday activity you can extend this mindfulness to is walking. Walking can be thought of as a metaphor for our mind and thoughts. Most of us walk without really being in the present moment, thinking instead of where we're headed toward, trying to get our steps in, or lost in worries or thought, instead of just being in the moment with our body, surroundings, and our senses. In our minds, we are also often rushing from thought to thought, just as we rush from place to place with our feet, thinking of the future, or worrying about the past, instead of just being present where we are. Instead of just being, just walking.

I've found I often receive answers when I'm outside walking. Being outside is helpful because it allows you to connect with nature and the earth, while walking mindfully or in a walking meditation helps better connects you with your body and inner wisdom. I have felt and heard answers come through very clearly on my walks, and often before I even finish getting my question out. Sometimes, the answers come through repeatedly, *Yes, yes, yes* or *No, no, no*. Try this walking meditation exercise, and then while you are present and calm, feel your heart center and bring up your question, ask it, and hold it in your heart. Allow yourself to feel open to any answer that may come, with no bias or preconceived notions. Then, listen and feel. Sometimes, the answers come through quietly, especially at first, when you are starting to tune into your inner wisdom and that of the universe around you.

The Work – Walking Meditation

Remember, as is the case with any meditation practice, walking or otherwise, when your mind wanders to a thought or distraction outside of your meditation, recognize it and let it go without any judgement or criticism, and then gently bring your mind back to the present and your meditation focus.

For your walking meditation, your focus is on your body and your senses. How does walking feel? Notice your steps, the sensations, and the movements. Notice how your body weight shifts from one leg to the other, shifting the weight from the back of your foot to the front of your foot, pushing off your back foot, and landing onto the next. How do your ankles, knees, and hip joints move and feel?

The purpose is to be in the present, with your body, with your movements, and with your senses. What do you feel, see, smell, and hear? You can choose to primarily focus on the sensations—the feelings of the walking movement for now, if you wish.

You can practice walking meditations inside or outside. You may wish to first practice inside. In the beginning, it may be helpful to practice walking slowly; however, choose the pace that feels best for you. Walking in nature or more natural surroundings can be helpful for you to connect more, but whatever is available to you is fine.

- Before you start walking, stand still, close your eyes, and turn your attention inward to your breath and body. Connect to your body and try to soften and relax it.

Then, start to slow your breathing, taking deep, intentional breaths. Stay there for as long as you wish before opening your eyes and starting your walk.

- As you start walking, move purposefully and intentionally. Be mindful of your movements. *I am lifting my right leg, placing the right heel down, pushing off the front of my right foot, and shifting the weight to my left leg and foot.*

- Keep tuning into your body, your legs, feet, and movements. Be in your body and embody yourself.

- Look one to two meters (three to seven feet) in front of your steps. Relax your shoulders and chest while keeping your spine and neck erect, yet relaxed. Hands and arms can be by your sides or clasped in front or behind. Whatever feels best for you.

- Try to walk for at least ten minutes, or as long as you wish. Once you finish your walking meditation, stand still, close your eyes, and turn your attention to your heart center. Notice how your body and heart center feel.

- Do your best to feel your chest relax, calm, and open and then, if you wish, ask a question while holding space in your heart center. Listen and feel. It is okay if you don't get an answer right away. The answer may come to you in another way or at another time. Now that you've asked and put the question out there, do your best to stay present as you go about your days and weeks, paying attention to messages and words that stand out to you.

Take as much time as you need in each meditation and coming out of the meditation. After each meditation, notice how you feel. Notice which meditations resonated with you or felt easy. I've outlined just a few meditations in this chapter, but there are many resources for meditation online, in books, and apps if you are curious to try others (see Resources for links to content I've created as well have enjoyed from others). I encourage you to try different meditations, and then practice the ones that resonate with you. The ones that feel easiest or that you're drawn to are the best to start with. In the beginning, my meditation was solely my yoga practice, and then it moved to body scans and chakra meditations. During my most stressful times, I found I gravitated toward mantra and loving-kindness meditations. To help detox and release, I often practice pranayama (breathing exercises). One is not better than the other, so, feel free to try different kinds, and then do the ones that feel best for you.

You may wish to write down your experience, or any thoughts or feelings that came up during your meditation. I highly recommend journaling coupled with meditation as a great process to work through the issues, questions, and answers in your life. The next chapter will delve deeper into this.

CHAPTER 4

Journaling

Allow your heart to tell you its story.

Lee Harris

WHEN WE WRITE freely, we allow our feelings to be expressed and to move through us. Sometimes, writing things out can be easier than saying them out loud. Growing up, I had several diaries. (I called them diaries when I was younger, and journals as I grew older.) I would often write when I felt angry, excited, frustrated, happy, sad, or lonely. I wrote whenever I was *feeling* my feelings. It was my safe space to let out all my private thoughts and feelings, helping me work through what I felt, but couldn't always verbalize out of fear, or articulate well in conversation. As I grew older and got busier with adult life, my journal writing became more sporadic, writing only when I was on vacation or going through very exciting or difficult times. Eventually, I stopped journal writing altogether for years, but kept my old journals. It was both comforting and interesting to read through them. After the cancer diagnosis, my husband and daughter bought me a new journal from the hospital gift shop while I rested after my resection surgery, which I now cherish as an inspirational gift. It took some time, but eventually, the words started flowing out again. In the beginning, my handwriting was messy because it had been a long time since I had written by hand. My handwriting remained messy as time went on, but it was because the words came falling out faster than I could write.

My journaling practice was an evolving journey. At first, I didn't feel like writing every day; however, I knew that journaling was a good practice, so, I kept my journal and a pen on my nightstand and tried to write before bed, even if it was just a few words. When I wasn't sure what to write, especially in the beginning as I re-established this habit, I simply wrote a list of what I was grateful for. Sometimes, I wrote affirmations like, "I am healthy" and "I am worthy", trying to work on actively shifting my mindset. Once I started meditating regularly again, it felt natural to write afterward, and the words started pouring out of me. As I progressed in my meditation practice and connecting within, the words started changing. I received messages that came through my writing, encouraging me, guiding me, and loving me. While it may be hard for some to believe, I was channeling these messages from my higher self (my energy, spirit, soul, or whatever word resonates with you), and other higher beings who support and guide me. It has evolved into a practice that has given me insight, comfort, guidance, and wisdom, and I know it is accessible for everyone else, as well. In my writing practice now, I connect within and write about my feelings and experiences, while also seamlessly connecting to my higher self, guides, and others. There is a collective intelligence I am consciously connected to.

I recommend writing in your journal after you've had an opportunity to ground and center yourself, perhaps after meditating, walking, yoga, exercising, or another activity where you're able to connect within and feel more at peace. It can even just be sitting for a few moments, quiet and still, breathing deeply, before opening your journal to write. I also suggest taking a moment to find your heart center before you write. This means feeling and connecting to the space inside your body, in the center of your chest, behind your breastbone/sternum. Feel this space and just relax and breathe slowly for a few breaths. If it feels right for you, you can also ask your higher self, guides, angels, light family, divine—whomever you wish—to share any messages that are for your greatest and highest good before you start to write. It may be helpful to gently ask your ego to step aside first before calling in other energies to channel.

Often, when I write and channel, I find that there is a lot of repetition. This may not be everyone's experience, but for me, the repetition reaffirmed these messages weren't coming from my mind. The messages have changed as I progressed and time passed; however, in the beginning, and for a long while, the words I wrote most often were "love love love love love love love yourself." Before I even thought of or consciously felt like writing this book, I often channelled the words "write write write write write" and "write your story" or "write a book" in my journal. That said, I did not start writing because I got those messages; in fact, at first, I didn't even feel like writing a book.

What I didn't realize at that time, however, was that my journal writing was also part of my book writing.

As you start to tune in and receive messages, be true to yourself. Don't do something just because you hear it from someone else; you need to feel it, and to want to do it for yourself. Don't feel that you need to always listen to other voices. You have to feel the best choice for you using your free will. And once you decide, trust that it is the right decision at that time. There are no wrong answers. You are the one that lives with the effects of any decision you make, and no one else can truly know all you feel and experience. Thus, no one else can make a better choice for you than yourself.

I sat with the idea of writing a book for months, and as time passed, I started to come around to the idea and feeling of writing a book, of sharing my story, experiences, and guidance in the hope that it helps others. My life goal has always been to help others live happier and healthier lives, and I recognized that this was another way to do just that. One day, I spontaneously decided to sit down and create a book outline, and it came together effortlessly within ten minutes. Afterwards, I smiled broadly and clapped my hands at my own accomplishment, like a toddler who had just discovered a new skill. The joy I felt in that organic moment showed me I was onto something.

Journaling Benefits

Expressing your thoughts, feelings, and experiences in writing can help you process and release what you've been through—or the things you've suppressed or held onto—and help lead you to your next step or answer. As you recount your experiences, you'll see that you're able to step back and look at them while no longer being immersed in the moment. This new perspective can help you see things you weren't able to see before, gain greater awareness, and give you more confidence or comfort in the decisions you make next.

Just as it can be a form of healing and release to talk out your feelings and thoughts with someone, you can do the same with your journaling practice. I've used my journal to write out pros and cons lists, and allow myself to let out streams of thoughts as I analyzed decisions to determine the best course of action for me. If you're wrestling with a critical life decision, writing out your options and thoughts can help you sort through them and decide what to do next. Additionally, scientific studies on journaling have shown that this practice can improve your mood, boost your well-being, reduce stress, and improve your memory. By better managing your stress through writing, it's also been demonstrated that journaling decreases symptoms of various health conditions, improves cognitive functioning, and strengthens your immune system.[19]

From the ancient Chinese perspective of *qi*, which can be described as life force energy, this is understandable as the practice of journaling helps you move stagnant energy, or *qi*. Based on ancient Eastern philosophies, and modern quantum physics, everything is made of life force energy or *qi* (also known as *prana*, *chi*, *ki*). Everything that you see and don't see is made of *qi*. It is in the air we breathe, the food we eat, the land we live on, and the bodies we live in. There is *qi* running through you and all around you. In traditional Chinese medicine, it is believed that you are healthy when your *qi* is flowing smoothly and easily. Conversely, ailments and illnesses are caused by the dis-ease of energy (*qi*) flow. Symptoms of illnesses are due to blocked, stagnated, or imbalanced *qi*, which can lead to dis-ease. We can move stagnated *qi* through various means, such as meditation, breath work, yoga, tai chi, qigong, journaling, and more. When we journal about our feelings and past traumas, we are tapping in and connecting to emotions or energies that may be blocked or stagnated. Recognizing and processing this blocked *qi*, energies, and emotions through journaling can allow us to let them go so they can flow freely, thus becoming more balanced and healthier.

The Work – Assess Your Options

Go back to The Work you did in Chapter 1 on Creating Your Compass, where you defined the kind of life you want to live. If you didn't do the exercise, I encourage you to do so now in your journal. You're going to use that answer as your guide, just as I did when I was deciding whether to quit a lucrative, "good on paper" job where I worked long hours. Using the life compass that I had created for myself helped me face the difficult reality that my seemingly successful job wasn't worth the trade-off of my health and time. While I only considered my physical and mental health at that time, I later came to realize it was also impacting my spiritual health. During a flight home from one of many draining work trips, I used the back of my boarding pass to assess my options and come to my answer. I wrote my life goals at the top, my options below, along with pros and cons of each option. I treated myself like a client and used similar strategies and thinking to guide my life decision-making that I would employ when advising clients. After I assessed what I wrote, the answer became glaringly clear.

Goals: To be happy. To be healthy. To have a positive impact on everyone who crosses my path. Question: Should I quit my job?			
Yes		No	
Pros	Cons	Pros	Cons
– less stress, more relaxed – healthier, more time to sleep, practice yoga, exercise – can find another job, done it before – supports and aligns with my life goals	– loss of income – walk away from a good job and title – career impact? unknown	– keep a steady and good income – career status quo	– remain stressed, unhappy and unhealthy – less quality time with Dave, friends and loved ones – doesn't support my life goals

Now, it's your turn. Using paper or an electronic device, open to a new page and put the life goals you outlined and distilled in the Chapter 1 exercise at the top. Underneath, write the question you are contemplating, and then in the left column, list each possible answer option, one per row. For each option, list the pros and cons and fill in the columns. Review what you filled in, and then for each option, assess whether that answer helps you move closer to your life goals or takes you further away from your goals and the life you want to live. Don't hold back. Write everything down, knowing that this is only for you. So, write from your heart, and don't be afraid to bare your truth. When you're finished, take a breath and review what you wrote.

	Pros	Cons	Does this answer help me to achieve or bring me closer to my life goals?
Life Goals: *List the life goals you've defined to help guide you in leading the life you want to live. This is the compass you defined in Chapter 1.* **Question:** *Write out the question that you are contemplating.*			
Option 1: *List a potential answer for the question you wrote above.*			
Option 2: *List a potential answer for the question you wrote above.*			
Option 3: *List a potential answer for the question you wrote above.*			

Take your time and allow it all to sink in. Is it obvious which answer is the right one for you? Which answer brings you closer to the life you want to live? Which answer is your life compass pointing you toward? How does that answer feel?

Know that there is a difference between knowing what's best for you and being ready for it. Give yourself space and time if you need it. It may feel scary to choose what is best for you, or to put yourself first. However, know that when you choose what's best for you, it is ultimately better for everyone else that may be affected by that decision, even if it may feel like the opposite of that at this moment. You cannot assume or choose how others will react to your decision. All you can do is the best for yourself. The easy answer isn't always the best answer. If you're unhappy in the life you're leading right now, will the easy answer give you more of the same or a chance for something new and different?

Unburden Yourself

Make time to journal regularly, even starting with just a couple of minutes a day. Journal when you have time, when you feel like it, when you're angry, when you're happy, when you feel like you've had a win, when you feel like you've had a loss, when you wake up in the morning, or before you go to bed. Reflect on your successes, accomplishments, failures, efforts, traumas, and joys. Write like no one else will ever read your journal. It is just for you.

Expressing yourself freely in your journal allows you to find and release your voice. Many people don't always feel supported, safe, or comfortable expressing themselves freely, and don't feel as though they can give voice to what they are truly feeling in their hearts, minds, and bodies. This stifling of your voice can lead you to feel more unsure about yourself, and less confident in making the right decisions for yourself. Our throat chakra—the energy in and around our throat—is open when we express and voice our truth. If you're feeling uncomfortable sharing it out loud with others, start with yourself and your journal.

Expressing your feelings unencumbered has been proven to be therapeutic. It is a cathartic process that enables you to acknowledge the feelings you've held and may not have been able to previously express without fear. By getting those feelings out in your journal, you are acknowledging them and allowing that energy to flow through you, rather than being repressed, suppressed, or denied. Even if you feel there is no one you can talk to about what you're going through and feeling, you have yourself, your words, and your journal. Allowing the expression of those feelings, thoughts, and experiences to pour out of you onto your journal gives them permission to be, an acknowledgment that it's okay to feel or think that way. Your feelings are your feelings. They are not right or wrong. They are simply feelings. Your experiences are your experiences. Your story is yours alone, unique yet familiar to others. Let it out. Use a notebook, paper, laptop, or phone. Dictate it into a voice recorder, if you prefer—just get it out. What you do afterwards is up to you. The process of recognizing and expressing those experiences and feelings can start to open your perspective.

Please do your best not to be judgemental of your writing, feeling, or thoughts. Simply allow yourself to express whatever it is you're feeling. It is not right or wrong to feel a certain way;

it just is, and by allowing yourself to have that space to be and to feel, you allow that energy to flow through you. Sometimes, we place such significance on thoughts and feelings that we cause ourselves unnecessary stress and anxiety. Sometimes, a thought is just a thought. A feeling is just a feeling. A judgement is just a judgment. Let them be. Try not to get attached to them. By letting them flow, you allow them to pass.

Reviewing your past journal entries can help give you greater perspective on what has happened over the weeks, months, and years, guiding you on your journey forward. Read your journal entries and see if you start to notice any patterns. I remember reading past journal entries and discovering that I wrote about the same issues many years apart, showing that little had changed in my mind regarding my concerns. That perspective gave me something to think about. Had things really not progressed and changed in the years I had first written about my insecurities and concerns? Or was that how I was choosing to look at things? I found it interesting that while circumstances in my life had definitely shifted, my writing didn't show progression in my perspective. Reading past entries can be eye-opening, comforting, captivating, and engaging. It can help you gain greater awareness and lead to more growth, and it is a practice I suggest you engage in often.

Perhaps, upon reviewing and reflecting on your words, you notice you no longer feel the hot flashes of anger or grief, even if just a subtle decrease. With time, perhaps you may wonder why such an issue even bothered you so much. Perhaps you start to see what choices led to those experiences, and how you can choose differently in the future. In looking back, we can move further ahead without tripping over the same obstacles. History is studied for several reasons, and often acts as a reminder of the factors that led to atrocities of war and conflict, and as a reminder of what is possible. Just as our societies can learn from history, we can learn from introspection. In that introspection, new truths and realizations can emerge, so that we may step around or over similar obstacles in the future.

Your journal writing is a chance for you to speak your truth, be your authentic self, and allow any and all feelings and experiences to be acknowledged and come through. To allow yourself to fully feel, and to be. And in that allowance, you enable the energy of the feelings and experiences to move as they were meant to. To reflect and learn from them as you look back and remember. To expand your perspective and let go.

Tips:

- To express and write freely, you need to feel that your writing is private and confidential. Your journal is for you and you alone. If you wish to share parts of it with others, that's up to you; however, write for yourself, unencumbered.

- Center yourself before writing. This can be as simple as taking a few, slow deeps breaths before starting, or doing a quick body scan meditation to recognize and release any tension you're holding onto and relax. I encourage you to couple your meditation and journaling practice together whenever possible, writing in your journal after you meditate when you are feeling calmer and more connected. These practices coupled together are empowering and life changing.

- Write in a space where you won't be disturbed and feel comfortable writing freely.

- Review your journal entries from time to time. Do your best to observe what you wrote while trying not to judge your writing or what you were feeling or experiencing at that time. Reading your past journal entries is a great way to see how you've grown and evolved, and to recall what you were experiencing at that time, and how things have changed from that moment. Experiences that may have resulted in strong emotions like anger, sadness, or frustration, sometimes fade, and recounting it through your journal writing can help you become more aware and gain greater perspective.

- Let it all out. Let the emotions pour through you and onto paper. This action can help you acknowledge and process the feelings you have, while also helping energy flow more freely, instead of getting stuck and harbouring in your body.

- Write on paper, on a laptop, mobile phone or even use a voice recorder. Use whatever medium feels best and easiest for you. If you are writing, feel free to also draw pictures if that feels right for you, as that can help in expressing your energy and emotions.

- Aim to journal a few times a week or even daily. Journaling frequently is a wonderful practice to help you process and release daily emotions and experiences.

These days, I write in my journal after my morning meditation practice; however, when I first started journaling, the words weren't flowing as freely, so, I kept my journal by my bed to write before going to sleep. Even if it was just a few sentences a day, writing an affirmation or gratitude before I went to sleep helped me establish a regular journaling practice.

- Don't forget to write the date at the beginning of your journal entry.

As you write freely and expressively, you allow your energetic self to recognize and release the emotions that have stayed with you from your experiences. The more present you are, the less energetic residue will stay with you as you acknowledge what is happening and allow those emotions and experiences to move freely. Most of us, however, are not yet present all the time. With time, journaling allows you to release the low frequency emotions that you've been carrying around with you—like fear, sadness, anger, guilt, anxiety, frustration, hatred—and enables you to be freer and feel higher frequency energies and emotions more easily—like joy, peace, gratitude, freedom, and love.

Your journal is yours. Write about whatever you wish. You may have concerns about others finding and reading your journal, so, do your best to safeguard your writing if you feel vulnerable. You may even choose to destroy some of your journal pages afterward if you're really concerned. When I was younger, I kept my journal in a lock box, and sometimes changed names or used codes for fear of others finding my journal. Though it may not have been necessary, it allowed me to write freely.

As you start to move your energy, release, and let go of what you no longer need through your writing process, you will start to peel back the layers. You will shed layers that have been built up around you as you have gone through life, peeling back the layers until you reach your core self. The more you can process, feel, and eventually let go of those events and emotions you've held onto, the closer you'll get to your inner self, and the easier it will be to hear your inner wisdom and find your answers. You'll be able to hold your answers in your heart center and know what is best for you at that moment. If you're ready to give journaling a try, but aren't sure where to start, here are three ideas to get you going: gratitude, reflection, and dream journaling.

1. Gratitude

Research has shown that expressing gratitude helps you reach your goals, while also improving well-being and feelings of happiness.[20] When we are feeling grateful, we are lighter. Expressing gratitude is a useful prompt in journal writing. If you're finding it hard to establish a consistent journal practice, you can simply start with writing three to five things you're grateful for. You can do this at any time of the day; however, I found it helpful to have my journal by my bed to write briefly before sleep when I was re-establishing a journaling practice. Expressing gratitude instantly shifts your mood. It can be a quick practice that takes a couple of minutes; however, I encourage you to take your time and feel your gratitude as you reflect and write.

My daughter and I often practice expressing three things we're grateful for at bedtime. At first, she viewed it as a chore, repeating quickly and monotonously the same three things each night so she could get it over with: "I'm grateful for my family, food, and house." Then, I took an approach in which I expressed gratitude first, taking my time to explain and describe what I was feeling. I found that afterwards, she followed up with a more organic gratitude response of her own, usually about something she experienced that day. No matter what she said, I did my best not to judge because they were her feelings and experiences. When you write your gratitude, anything goes. Do not worry about being superficial and try not to judge or criticize your writing.

2. Recount and Reflect

Many of my journal entries simply recount and reflect on the experiences from that day or the days prior. Recounting your experiences, feelings, and thoughts can help you sort and process all that has transpired. You get a chance to let out feelings that you felt and may or may not have expressed at that time. Recounting and reflecting your experiences in your journal writing can also help you become more self-aware and organize your thoughts. When you are writing in your journal, you are outside of the experience that occurred. This time and space can enable you to adopt other perspectives on the experience that you may not have been able to see at that moment. The act of thinking about, summarizing, and expressing what happened and how you felt helps you process that experience, moving that energy instead of having it lay stagnant. The more you can reflect, process, accept, and let go of what has happened, the more you free yourself of emotional baggage, blocks, and stagnated energy. Even when you believe there is no one to confide in, there is: yourself. Journaling is a powerful tool that can help you heal, letting go of energy and experiences that have caused pain or illnesses. Allow the words to flow through you onto your journal pages, off your chest and shoulders.

3. Dream Journaling

When we dream, our minds or subconscious may be processing events from the day or past. Often, we recall our dreams as seemingly random or weird experiences; however, if we take some time to dig a little deeper, we may find messages and answers within. If you are struggling to arrive at an answer to a decision, you can try posing the question before bed, and paying attention to your dream recollection when you wake up in the morning, writing it down in your journal. Before you go to bed, write the question down in your journal, hold it internally in your heart center, and then let go of it and go to sleep. When you awake, before you get up and start your day, stay still and try to recall any dreams you may have had. Write down what you remember in your journal. You may find that you got an answer in your dream. By asking the question before bed, you are putting it out there—into your subconscious mind, the universe, to others, and so on—and then listening, observing, or interpreting the answers that may come through in your subconscious mind through your dreams. In Chapter 7, I share a story of how I used this exercise to land on a critical answer regarding which oncologist to choose for surgery after wrestling with the question for a while.

Dream journaling can be a helpful practice, even without posing any questions. Keeping your journal beside your bed and writing as soon as you wake up can be helpful to remember your dreams before they fade away. Or you can write about the dreams you recall later in the day. Writing down your seemingly odd, random, and memorable or fleeting dreams can be a good way to help you start processing and interpreting them. Dream interpretation will be explored more in Chapter 7.

Automatic Writing

A few years ago, a mentor of mine suggested that I try automatic writing, which I hadn't heard of before. I looked it up and learned it was about tuning in and allowing whatever scribbles or words to come out of you freely. I decided to try it. I tuned in, took a few deep breaths to connect within, while holding a pen poised over a writing pad. I allowed whatever wanted to flow out of me to come out. They were all indecipherable scribbles. I didn't judge and left it. I tried again another time, tuning in, and allowing myself to write continuously, even closing my eyes at times. I scribbled indecipherably for over half a page, and then I noticed that the same patterns were being drawn over and over again. They started to become clearer each time until they revealed to me the legible words of "do yoga." Over and over again, "do yoga do yoga do yoga do yoga do yoga" was scribbled clearly by the end of the page. I put my pen down and was taken aback.

I found the message in the writing interesting, as I had been practicing yoga for over fifteen years at that point, with large ebbs and flows in my practice. At that time, I was at a low ebb, not practicing much at all. I started practicing again, along with daily meditation. It was instrumental in my healing, to move stagnant energy within and around me. My practice evolved from a familiar yoga practice to an intuitive yoga and energy movement meditation. I would come to my mat daily, breathe deeply, connect, and become heart centered. I fully embodied myself, and then allowed my body and energy to move how it needed and wanted to. As time passed, my intuitive practice evolved. Sometimes, it looked like a yoga practice, and other times, it looked like tai chi, martial arts, or a spiritual dance. My breathing also changed, at times going into a detox breath, letting out sounds from my mouth with the back of my throat constricted and moving into various pranayama breath work practices. There was a phase when I would hum. I startled my family with loud spontaneous clapping. I tapped on acupressure points, or in circles and figure eights around my chakras. Often, my practice organically ended in a sitting meditation. I let my body move any way it wanted to, and I always knew when my practice was finished. Afterward, I always felt cleansed and rejuvenated. Any day that I missed my intuitive practice, I noticed a difference in my mood.

Notice How Your Treat Yourself

It can be an eye-opening experience to read your past journal entries, and to see what you were feeling and experiencing from a new perspective. Charged emotions and situations you felt at that time may have been forgotten and faded in significance as time passed. Reviewing your journal entries can also give you a chance to be more objective. Is what you wrote in the past *really* true? Do you know these as facts or beyond a shadow of a doubt? Did your worries come to fruition, or did they simply cause unnecessary stress?

Reading your old journal entries can also show you patterns in your thinking and self-talk. How are you treating yourself in your journal writing? How do you talk to yourself? Is there criticism, judgement, and negative self-talk in your words? Or are you optimistic, hopeful, and compassionate with yourself? It can be revealing to review and see how you're treating yourself. Look at how you are treating yourself in your journal writing, and consider how you would feel if your child (or a loved one) shared their journal with you and they treated themselves in a similar manner. Would you be pleasantly surprised that they had a healthy sense of awareness, worth, and self-love? Or would you feel that they were hard on themselves and surprised that they talked to themselves in such a negative and critical voice?

Reading your journal entries can reveal patterns in whether you are treating yourself with love and kindness, or judgement and anger. If you wouldn't want your child or loved one to be writing about themselves in a similar manner, it's a good sign to evaluate why you may be treating yourself this same way. The inner work shared in the next chapter will give you a chance to delve deeper into the mirror you are now holding up to yourself.

CHAPTER 5

Address Your Blocks

It is your attitude,
more than your aptitude,
that will determine your altitude.

Zig Ziglar

FOR MOST OF my life, I judged my value and self-worth based on what I achieved. It took me until I was almost forty years old to realize that this was a blind spot, fully accepting that I am not defined by my job. I am not defined by what I do or achieve. I finally understand now that my job is not my identity. I am more. We are all more.

However, many of us were—and still are—unconsciously conditioned to believe that our job or what we do is our identity. Think about when you meet people for the first time. Often, the question, "So, what do you do?" comes up, and you may feel that the other person is judging you based on your answer. Growing up, I instilled in myself that I needed to constantly achieve to *make it* in life. This ultimately meant having enough of my own money so I would never need to worry or rely on anyone else, which was important to me growing up in a household with serious debt and money issues due to a parent with a gambling addiction and another who turned a blind eye. From my upbringing and society, I was indoctrinated to believe a simple formula: good grades in school = lucrative career as an adult = life success. Anything else was failure.

From the time I started school to when I graduated from university, I put a lot of stress and pressure on myself to achieve, achieve, achieve, so I could ultimately get a "good" job that would define success in my life. One that would show others that *I made it*. However, getting good grades, going to a good school, and landing a good job involved more than just studying. I didn't really need to study much throughout high school because most subjects came easily. I spent a lot more time working part-time and in extracurricular activities than on schoolwork and studying. I knew that getting into a good school and university program meant more than high grades; they wanted well-rounded students. I was the newspaper editor, a Prefects leader, spent countless hours on the yearbook committee, part of the UN council, orchestra, and sports teams. I was all over the yearbook in team or group activity photos. Outside of school, I also volunteered my time assisting numerous charities and mentoring other kids.

But what I remember most was working. I started working part-time as soon as I was able to—at thirteen years old. My first paid job was working at a department store as a customer care representative. After that came jobs in a childcare center, supermarket, another department store, banks, and in a bar as a bartender (even though I didn't drink alcohol). While in university, on top of my full course load, I worked forty hours/week across three part-time jobs. Commuting to and from school took two and a half hours daily, and then I also had to commute to my jobs on top of that. Needless to say, I was tired, stressed, and not taking care of myself.

I often nodded off while studying and in class. But I told myself I had to work so much because I had to pay for school, and I harboured a healthy fear of debt from my childhood. No one else was going to pay for my education, and I knew that from a very young age, which fuelled my intent to work the hours I did. As a young child, I witnessed family circumstances that made me internalize the belief that I would never be able to rely on anyone else, financially or otherwise. I had to succeed for me, because no one else was going to take care of me (and I wouldn't let them). So, I worked, a lot, and all the time.

Fast-forward eighteen years, and I'm lying on the couch in my house, on medical leave from work, recovering from my resection surgery for the colon cancer diagnosis I had been recently dealt. For six weeks, I was supposed to take it easy as my body recovered, and yet there I was, looking at the kitchen and internally berating myself for "being lazy" because I wasn't cleaning, cooking or *doing* anything. It didn't matter that I just had major surgery. I had equated *working*, *doing* and *achieving* with my identity and self-worth for my whole life, and so, in my mind, I was being lazy, and that didn't feel good. That was a catalyst to my journey of addressing my blocks and inner work. It took a lot of internal examination, self-care, empathy, releasing, forgiving, and self-love, along with yoga, meditation, and journaling, to get to a place of understanding and acceptance that I wasn't lazy, that my value wasn't equated to what I *did*. From there, I was empowered to live in more of my truth, which included quitting my job, turning down an executive role with a "great" title, and instead choosing to continue healing and working on myself, which would have been unfathomable to me just months earlier, as my identity was so wrapped up with my corporate career. After that, it became easy for me to take time for myself to recharge and rejuvenate. I no longer felt any shame in answering the "so, what do you do?" question, even without an executive job title to reply with.

Now, I understand that the formula I believed growing up (good grades in school = lucrative career as an adult = life success) is not true. Instead, I resonate with a more reliable formula derived from one of author and motivational speaker, Zig Ziglar's sayings: *attitude = altitude*. This chapter is about changing your attitude and opening yourself to more inner wisdom and answers by addressing your blocks. Just like I criticized myself for lying on the couch doing "nothing" while recovering from surgery, you have blocks that are preventing you from seeing the full picture and treating yourself with the love and kindness you deserve. These blocks and limiting beliefs have been with you for a long time, running in your mind on auto-pilot. So, it's going to take internal examination, effort, and time to overcome and release these. But you can do it, because if I can go from calling myself lazy while recovering from major surgery to happily allowing myself to watch tv and take day-time naps for self-care, you can certainly address your blocks as well. By addressing them, you'll also open yourself to your inner wisdom and best answers. Like you, I was living unconsciously with limiting beliefs and attitudes. However, once I recognized and changed them, not only was I happier, but I also gained more access to my intuition and energy. Doing the inner work—as described in this chapter and book—to reveal and mitigate your blind spots will bring you closer to your best answers.

Treat Yourself with Kindness

Many of us have a running commentary going on in our monkey minds with an endless chatter of thoughts running into one another. If you stop and bring your awareness to your thoughts, you'll likely notice that many of those thoughts aren't very kind. They may show up when you try to do something you enjoy, telling you that "you should be working, cleaning, or more productive instead." Once you start bringing your awareness to your thoughts, you may find that they're judgmental, saying, "You should do this", "why didn't you do that", "you're so stupid", or "you don't deserve that". Listen to the voice objectively and you'll find that many of the comments are criticisms and limiting beliefs or attitudes developed over time that you may have assumed *are* you, as you identified with them. But you are not your thoughts. ***You are not your thoughts.*** That critical, judgmental voice is not you. That voice can change. It can become much quieter, and you'll still be here, feeling better than ever.

The most important relationship you have in this lifetime is with yourself. I want you to remember this. The way you talk to and treat yourself is the most important relationship you'll ever have, and it will impact every other relationship and interaction you have in your life. So, treat yourself with kindness. Talk to yourself like you would want your child to talk to themselves. How would you feel if you heard your child or loved one constantly berating themselves? It would be heartbreaking, yet you're doing the same to yourself every day, and it doesn't have to be this way, nor is it helpful.

Imagine a baby or newborn infant. I want you to picture their chubby, cute cheeks and face. Now, do they deserve to be loved? Of course. Do they need to do anything to earn that love? Is there anything they could do to no longer deserve being loved? Of course not. It is easy for us to see and understand that every baby deserves to be loved, and they don't have to do anything to earn it, nor can they do anything to lose it. They deserve to be loved and have all the opportunities in the world just for being. As that baby grows up, at what point do they no longer deserve to be loved? As our children age, at what point do they no longer deserve to be unconditionally loved? When they get a bad grade at school? When they throw a temper tantrum? When they make a mistake? Never. Well, we were all those babies, and we still deserve to be treated with love just for being. And there is *nothing* we need to do to earn that love, nor is there anything we could do to no longer deserve being loved. As we grew older, at what point did we no longer deserve to be unconditionally loved? Never. Treat yourself with loving kindness in your thoughts, words, feelings, and actions because you deserve it.

It is not selfish to give to yourself
first before giving to others.
It's self-care.

Enjoy Life

Start by enjoying the life you have right now. No one's life is perfect, and even if your life is far from perfect, there are still things you can do to find moments of peace—or even joy—every single day. Start with one little thing. Do things that you enjoy and make you feel good, even if you can only find a few minutes at a time. This could be basking in the sunshine, going for a walk, spending time with your kids without worrying about what else you need to get done, getting a massage, listening to music, singing out loud, dancing around the house, and so on. Whatever it is, do something that makes you feel better and lifts your mood. I'm not talking about activities that are vices where you feel good in the moment due to escapism and then crash and feel worse later. Instead, these are activities that leave you feeling lighter and more relaxed, where you smile more and frown less. And what's important is that you do it without feeling guilty, or disparaging, judging, and criticizing yourself. Just enjoy, be in the moment, and know that you deserve it.

Be Present

Being kind to yourself and having the awareness when a critical thought arises requires presence. It has been found that most of us are thinking about what is not happening almost as much as we are thinking about what *is* happening at that moment. In a November 2010 study called, *A Wandering Mind is an Unhappy Mind* from Harvard University, Matthew A. Killingsworth and Daniel T. Gilbert found that when people thought about what wasn't happening—meaning their minds were not in the present and instead in the past or future—they were typically unhappy. They concluded that "a human mind is a wandering mind, and a wandering mind is an unhappy mind." However, it doesn't have to be this way. While it is normal and natural for our minds to wander—our minds are in Default Mode Network when this occurs—we have the ability to retrain our minds and redirect our thoughts.[21] When the monkey mind is chattering, our thoughts are wandering, and that inner voice is going on, often worried about the future or concerned with the past, or daydreaming of a situation that hasn't happened, thus not engaged in the present—the Default Mode Network is active in the brain. These thoughts, ruminations and worries can trigger our sympathetic nervous system, and activate the fight, flight, or freeze response, meaning stress hormones are pumping through our bodies in anticipation of helping us deal with a threat. Most of the time, however, there is no real, external, life or death threat; our thoughts alone cause the stress. Mindfulness, meditation, and being present helps shift our brain away from Default Mode Network and activate our parasympathetic nervous system so we are in the rest and digest mode. Being present removes ourselves from the regretful past we are replaying, or the uncertain negative future scenario we're imagining, and brings us back to now, where we actually are.

When you're taking time to do the things you enjoy, do your best to be fully present and there to enjoy it, instead of thinking about what else you need to do or "should" be doing. All we ever have is the moment we're in right now. Yet, many of us use that time to worry or stress about the past or future, and when that future we were concerned about comes around, we're still not there, because we're in another future or past instead of the present. So, when you wake up in the morning, be present instead of looking at your phone or worrying about the day ahead. When you brush your teeth in the morning, be present instead of thinking about what you're going to wear or do next. When you're taking a shower, be in the shower, feel the water, and focus on where you are and what you're doing. When you are commuting, be present instead of thinking about your upcoming meetings or to-do list. And when you have the awareness that your mind has wandered from the present moment, gently guide it back, with no criticism.

When I was in my second year of university, I had an epiphany. It came at a low point when I was unhappy, unhealthy, and exhausted. I woke up one day from a nap I'd taken in the library when I was supposed to be studying and suddenly thought, *What if I died tomorrow? What would this all have been for? I've been living and working for the future for so long, but what if it never comes and I die? I would have spent my whole life up to now living and working for a future that never came.* I decided then and there that I would start living more in the present, vowing not to have any regrets in life. It was freeing. While I didn't change completely overnight, and still worked a lot for fear of not having enough money and needing to be independent, it was a turning point in my life. My singular goal of graduating from university to attain a solid career expanded to also include wanting balance in my life, both now and in the future, and having quality time to spend on activities I enjoyed and being with people I loved.

You are retraining and rewiring your brain when you become aware and constantly bring yourself back to the present—when you choose to stop worrying about the future or the past and turn your thoughts and attention instead to the present and where you are now. While this sounds like a simple concept, it will take awareness and consistent effort as you are breaking habits that have been ingrained in you your whole life, if not longer. Be patient with yourself, remember to treat yourself with kindness, try not to criticize yourself, and know that you're doing your best, and that is enough. You are enough.

Fuel the Way You Want to Live

Look at your thoughts and feelings as fuel or energy. What you think about, feel, and do is what you're fuelling. You're putting energy into whatever that is. So, if you constantly have negative thoughts, fears, worries, anxieties, and concerns, you're feeding those thoughts and feelings with fuel, and increasing the likelihood of bringing them to you. Conversely, if you have loving, kind, joyful, and empathetic thoughts and feelings, that is what you're fuelling and will bring into your life.

If you want to feel better, start feeling better. This takes work, but you have a choice—we all do. Most of us allow that choice to be made for ourselves unconsciously and believe that there is nothing we can do about it. But we are in control. This isn't necessarily easy when you're just getting started, but it gets easier. The first step is to set your intention. How is it that you want to feel? What do you want to bring into your life, and how will that make you feel? Find and set that intention. Many people will say, "I want to be rich or wealthy." Now think about how that would make you feel. Free? Never needing to worry about money? Abundant? Those are the feelings to hold on to, to fuel and energize you.

Awareness comes next. You need to be aware of what you are thinking, what is running through your mind, and how your body feels. If it is not how you want to feel, then once you notice it, change it. It's important at this point not to criticize or judge yourself for feeling or thinking what you were. Just notice without judgement. And then, shift it to how you want to feel, and where you want to fuel your energy. Once you become aware, there is no turning back; however, you can move forward and change.

Then, repeat. Over and over again. At first, this may seem like a never-ending cycle of negative thoughts and feelings coming up, but if you keep noticing them without judgement, letting them go and then bringing your mind back to the present, or even redirecting your thoughts to how you want to feel, you are doing The Work. You're building the neural pathways and connections in your body and brain, and over time, it'll get easier. Recognize what you're feeling and what thoughts are coming up, but do not get attached to them. Let them go. Then, you can choose to bring in a feeling that you want more of in your life, or simply bring your awareness back to the present, maybe noticing your breath, body, or heart to help you stay present instead of in your thoughts.

The Work – Let It All Out

To connect within and get answers, it's best to deal with the emotions, situations, and feelings you may have repressed in respect to the question, and have held over your lifetime. The more you allow yourself to feel—to just be with your feelings without judging them or yourself—the easier it'll be to release them and let them pass through you. Your feelings and emotions are energies that want to be expressed and move, and when you don't allow yourself to do that, they can get stuck or build up, making it more difficult to access the peace within that brings you the best answers for your greatest good.

You are your own best teacher, guide, and coach. Yet it's very easy to get in your own way, which most of us do. By allowing yourself to feel your emotions, process them fully, and let them go, you help clear the hurdles in front of you—the challenges you've laid. You clear a more direct path to your inner self, and the conscious intelligence that has your best interests at heart, helping you answer your critical questions with love. This takes time and effort, but I promise that it's worth it. Try to do the following every day, or as often as you can:

- **Move Your Body** - Start by tuning in to yourself. Be in your body, allow it to feel, and to relax. Allow it to let go of the tension you've been carrying around for so long. Move your body and feel. Stretch, walk, dance, practice yoga, and so on. Do whatever feels good. Allow your body to move intuitively, unencumbered, and do what feels natural.

- **Breathe into it and Let it Out** – Breathe deeply. Our breath helps to move the energy around us, including energies that may be stuck or blocked. Slowly inhale through your nose, filling up your diaphragm and lungs, then, exhale it all out through your nose just as slowly. Repeat multiple times until you feel more relaxed.

- **Tune In** - What do you notice? What can you feel? Can you sense the energy inside your body? Look at your hand, move it around, and sense the energy inside. Now, close your eyes. Can you still sense the energy there? Try to sense the energy inside your hand, and all around your hand. Now, do that for each part of your body, starting from your feet, and moving all the way up to the top of your head, or reversed. Notice where it may be more difficult to sense or feel the energy inside or all around your body. That is a blockage. There is a resistance there from energy that has been stuck and repressed. Work on letting it go or simply notice it. Remember the Body Scan and Gratitude exercise from

Chapter 2 (this is essentially the same). Keep sensing the space, then add in loving kindness, love that space, and that body part. Forgive it. Tell yourself you are allowing yourself to feel and let go of what you no longer need. Bless that part of your body for your greatest health and good, and move onto the next body part.

- **Allow Yourself to Feel** - Allow yourself to process and feel whatever emotions there are that comes up daily. Feeling sad? Don't hold back the tears. Let them out. If you're feeling angry, don't bottle it up. Let the feelings out in a healthy way (i.e., don't attack someone with your feelings). Stomp your feet, take a fast walk or jog around the neighbourhood, punch a pillow, or journal about it. Whatever it is, when the emotions come up, allow them to come through you. Don't hold them back because you don't want them to get stuck. Once you've allowed them to pass, observe that the feelings have passed, and then choose where you are going to direct your thoughts and energy. What can you do to ground yourself, to center yourself, and to feel calmer? Turn inwards to your breath and body.

Do What Resonates with You

Try not to feel overwhelmed if it feels like there is a lot to remember and do from this chapter (and the book overall). You don't have to do it all at once. Take your time. Notice which words, suggestions, and exercises are resonating with you and just start with those. Reading these pages is one thing, but putting in effort and action is another. Do what feels right for you; however, don't be afraid to push yourself outside your comfort zone.

While you may not need to undertake all the steps shared in this book to get answers for your questions, the practices outlined will make it easier to always be open to answers that are in your best interest. This leads us to a powerful and challenging Forgiveness & Unburdening exercise that has impacted me greatly.

To forgive is to free yourself.
It is not about whether the other person has earned it,
rather, it is an act that allows you to let go of the space
and power that incident and person holds in your life.
When you can forgive and let go,
space opens for new things to come in.

The Work – Forgiveness, Letting Go, and Unburdening Exercise

Forgiveness is a gift you give to yourself. Holding onto grudges and anger while reliving the past takes you out of the present and where you are now. I harboured anger and resentment for years, and for a long time, my way of dealing with it was distance. I felt that if I distanced myself from the thoughts, people, and places that triggered me, that was enough. But that didn't mean the charged emotions went away. They were just buried. When I started to practice forgiveness, it brought a new sense of peace and empathy, and I've learned that it's not a one-time act. I've had to forgive, forgive, and forgive again to let go. The Work doesn't end, but it does get easier.

The purpose of this exercise is to help you forgive yourself and others to let go of the feelings and trauma that have burdened you. Forgiveness can be a weighty term, so, know that this has to feel right for you. No one is forcing you to forgive every person in your life that has knowingly or unknowingly inflicted pain on you in the past, but the one person I want you to try to forgive is yourself.

When you can forgive and let go, you make space for new things to enter. You will unburden yourself of all the space that old energy took holding onto the emotions, hurt, and grudges. Forgiveness doesn't change what anyone did, nor does it absolve them of it, but it will help you understand that they have their own lessons to learn, and it's not your job to ensure they apologize, repent, and change. Letting go is not about the other person; it's about you and allowing yourself to have peace of mind and space for new, better energies to come in. It doesn't make you any less to let go—quite the opposite, actually. It brings you more. More peace, more ease, more love. More. So, forgive, let go, unburden yourself, and repeat as often as needed to as many people and parties required to feel good, better, and more at peace. For most of us, fully forgiving and releasing is not achieved in one day. I had to do this exercise over and over and over again. And when I noticed that I was triggered, reacting negatively or with fear or anger toward one of these people, I tuned in and forgave again—both them and myself. You'll know you've forgiven when the anger is gone, and when the charged emotions that were buried no longer surface with just a mention of a name or story. When there are no more triggers, you've let go. When you can think of these people and incidents, separating the person from their actions, and can embrace them in your heart and mind, truly wishing them well.

All the traumatic and difficult memories that have stayed with you are still taking space and energy. The energy from those moments have imprinted on you, but you don't need to keep holding onto those difficult emotions. You can let go. Part of the process is allowing any feelings and emotions you've repressed to surface and pass before you can fully let go and unburden yourself. This will take time and a great deal of empathy, patience, and self-love. It may come on suddenly and unexpectedly, but when you're ready and open, the energies will surface to release. The Work in this chapter, and in previous chapters, was instrumental in my healing journey, especially daily mediation, being in my body through yoga, and journaling.

1. Write a list of all the people in your immediate family, and those closest to you. Include people from current and past significant relationships, as well as those you've had conflicts or difficult experiences with—anyone that may elicit a charged or negative emotion when you think of them, see them, or hear their name.

2. Go through each person on the list, one at a time. Can you accept what has happened with that person? Can you accept the reality of the situation? Can you accept no longer being in denial (if you were at any point)? Now, I ask that you accept that there is a lesson for you

to learn from the experiences with each of these people. What are the lessons? Write them down for each person. See if you notice any patterns in your answers. Are you able to learn from these experiences and move forward?

3. Add your name to the bottom of the list. Move down the list, and for each person, choose to forgive them and let go of the emotions you've been holding onto that have been stunting you and pulling you down. You may choose to do this by recording your thoughts, saying them out loud, saying them internally, picturing what it would look like to forgive them in person, or even forgiving them in person. For some people on this list, it will be easy, but for others, it will be hard, and you may find yourself resistant to this activity. Don't force yourself. Skip those people and keep going down the list. However, do your best to ensure that you at least forgive yourself. Tell yourself regarding all the experiences in your life, from past to present, that you love, accept, and forgive yourself. Feel love for yourself. Repeat this exercise as needed.

4. Take a few deep breaths, slowly inhaling and exhaling through your nose. Feel your lungs and diaphragm expand with air as you inhale, and slowly fall as you exhale. Once you feel calm, bring your awareness to your heart center, the space inside your body in the center of your chest, behind your breastbone, and in front of your spine. Keep your attention and awareness in this space. Notice how it feels. Try to soften it if you're

holding tension or tightness here. Breathe deeply. Say to yourself, internally or out loud, "I'm ready to let go of what I no longer need. I'm ready to let go of what is not for my greatest and highest good. I let go of and accept the past. I am letting go of what I no longer need." Repeat as many times as you wish.

5. Drink water and do something that makes you feel good, calmer, or more relaxed. Be gentle and easy with yourself.

Moving slowly gets you further than standing still.
Aim for progress, not perfection.

CHAPTER 6

Put It Out There

Ask and you will receive.

Jesus

I F YOU'VE PRACTICED the prior steps of meditation, connecting to your body, journaling, and doing your inner work consistently, and are still unsure what the right answer is, another step is to simply ask. Asking is a step that can be done in conjunction with all the practices shared from the previous chapters. You can ask your question and tune into your body for the answer, sensing how it reacts. Does it feel open and relaxed, indicating an affirmative response, or tight and closed up, responding with a "no, thank you"? You can ask for clarity on your question before you start to journal, or after you've centered yourself with meditation. You can ask your question while holding space in your heart center, and sensing what answers you receive in return. You can ask your question before you go to bed at night by writing it in your journal, saying it internally, or out loud. Ask, put your question out there, and then let go. Do not get attached to the question. Let it be and pay attention for any responses.

125

You can ask a question, or you can simply state what it is that you want. Keep in mind that while what you ask for is in your own best interest. It should not be a request that interferes with others and their own free will. Say what you need and put it out there into the universe (or divine, god, spirit, or whatever word resonates with you) to plant the seed. And just like a seed that has been planted, you must tend to it with water and care. Water and nourish your request (or question) with your own initiative and efforts, putting in the work that will help lead you to the best results. Do not hold on to the request, ruminating over it and analyzing. Simply let it be, just as seed needs to stay in the ground and be given time to germinate and grow. As your request is germinating and growing, you can help it come to fruition by imagining what it will feel, look, and taste like when ripe and ready to be plucked and consumed. How will it feel when your request has come true?

Perhaps you've already experienced this if you've had an instance when you casually mentioned something that you'd like to receive and sometime later, that very thing manifested for you. My husband is a masterful manifestor, proving his abilities several times over. He doesn't stress or dwell on issues, is very present, and trusts that things will always work out, and thus, is able to manifest easily. While his path has been different from mine, and he doesn't always understand everything I've experienced, the examples of manifestation we've experienced are something he cannot deny. A few years ago, as I was getting deeper into my spiritual journey, I was at my cousin's place, chatting after a Reiki session she had given me. It was a Friday afternoon, a few months after my resection surgery, and my understanding of energy was developing when the topic of manifestation came around and I asked her, "How do we manifest?"

"It's simple," she replied. "We can do an exercise right now. Just think of something you would like."

"A free Japanese meal," I replied easily.

"Okay, now, feel what it would be like to have that Japanese meal," she instructed. That was easy for me because it was getting close to dinner time, and I'd been craving Japanese food for a while. I pictured and felt what it would be like to eat it. "Now, we'll put a timeframe on it," she continued. I asked for it by the end of the weekend, two days from then.

"Now what?" I wondered.

"Let it go," she replied.

"That's it?"

"That's it."

I left shortly after, and as I walked to my car, my husband called to ask me to order sushi for dinner. We're regulars at a neighbourhood sushi restaurant, so, I placed an order there and went to pick up the food on my way home. When I got home and we opened the bags, we noticed that one of the items from our order was missing, and I immediately knew this was how I was going to get my free Japanese meal. My husband went back to let them know that there was a missing item in our order, and when he got home, I wasn't surprised when he told me they gave us free extra sushi rolls and a seaweed salad, as I already anticipated it. With a big smile on my face, I said, "That was fast." I told my husband about how I was trying to manifest a free Japanese meal just a couple of hours prior. Being a very rational person, he dismissed it as a coincidence, but I knew in my heart that it was an occurrence I had manifested.

To drive home the point that I could manifest, the universe gave me three more free Japanese meals, receiving four in total over four months. For my birthday, my husband made reservations for an omakase meal from a high-end Japanese restaurant. Shortly after he made those reservations and before my birthday dinner, a recommendation he gave his boss at work turned into a million-dollar plus bonus for his company, and in return, his boss told him to go out for a nice dinner and to charge it to work. Thus, free Japanese meal #2 was paid for by his company. A few weeks later, we were in Hawaii on vacation. We had just landed and were eating at one of the hotel restaurants, enjoying the beautiful atmosphere. We ordered a range of foods, including chicken sandwiches, fries, salad, sushi rolls, and more. As my husband took a bite out of the chicken sandwich, he bit into a metal tie that held part of the vegetables together and wasn't taken off when the food was prepared. We informed the staff who were very apologetic, and they brought us another sandwich. At the end of the meal when we went to pay, they informed us that the entire meal was on them. My sister-in-law and brother who we were eating with us, and knew my manifestation story, looked at me and said, "You manifested another free Japanese meal!" referring to the free sushi rolls from our dinner. And that wasn't the last free meal from that trip. A few days later, while lounging by the pool alone, my lunch order of sushi rolls was also fully comped after it took the restaurant a longer than normal time to fulfil the order when it was inadvertently lost. I didn't mind as I was simply lounging by the pool for the afternoon, but my brother later pointed out that it was another free Japanese meal as I had again ordered sushi.

This experience helped turn my husband from a manifestation skeptic into a believer, especially after he started to manifest easily for himself. For example, one day, he mentioned he wanted AirPods (wireless earbuds) for his phone, and that same day, he got an email asking him to participate in a quick corporate survey, after which he would receive free AirPods as compensation for his time! There had been more examples like this (he always gets a prime parking spot no matter how busy it is), and now, he will say out loud what he is manifesting, and it often comes true.

The universe is listening. There is more to this world than meets the eye, and if you ask for help, if you ask for guidance in the question you are seeking to answer, you will get it. What is key is understanding how to look for the answers, guidance, signs, and messages. They won't necessarily be obvious, audible, or appear immediately (although they can). Be open and stay open. Notice what you notice. Pay attention to what resonates with you, and what stays with you.

Shortly after my resection surgery, I was still eager to get on with my old life. As I gradually started to regain strength, I went for daily walks around the neighbourhood, and "Slow Down" signs on lawns (to remind drivers to slow down as children played in the area) seemed to pop out at me and stayed with me long after I passed them. My eyes were drawn to "Slow Down" bumper stickers on cars in my neighbourhood that I'd never noticed before in years of walking around the area. Not long after, I was telling one of my cousins about this as we were out walking, and a few minutes later, we passed by a "Slow" construction sign. I got the message; I knew what the universe wanted me to hear. Those words, messages, phrases, or sentences that resonate with you stay etched in your mind after you hear or see them. They are for you. There's a reason they stood out. This is just one way you can notice and receive messages, guidance, and answers.

In fact, I wrote this book because of guided messages I had received. For months, I was waking up every night between 2 am and 4 am. As my personal and spiritual development progressed, I learned that was the time when the veil was the thinnest. In other words, it was the time when it was easiest to connect to spirit, or the universe. One night, I couldn't fall back asleep after waking up yet again in the middle of the night, and so, I decided to ask if there was a message for me. Instantly, I was flooded with a download of this book. The title and what it was all about. Once that was done, I promptly went back to sleep. I didn't feel surprised or shocked from the message, just very matter-of-fact about it. I thought about the message in the days and weeks that followed, as I never had any ambitions to write a book prior to that, and I still wasn't sure if I wanted to. So, I sat with that message and continued doing other things in my life that felt right for me at the time and aligned with my life goals—teaching yoga and meditation. A few months later, the idea of writing a book had sunken in, permeated into my being, and I sat down to write an outline, which came together effortlessly in less than ten minutes. The joy I felt when I completed that book outline with ease showed me I was onto something.

And so, it began. Writing this book was another way to work toward my life goal of helping others be happier and healthier, by sharing my story and the knowledge I learned along the way. I continued to receive many more messages about writing and sharing my story, and this book is one of the results.

When you are unsure of what direction to take in life, ask. Although it may seem like we are alone at times—or all the time for some people—I assure you we are not. There is more than meets the eye. Ask your question, put it out there into the universe, and see how the universe responds. Observe the subtle responses you receive in the coming minutes, hours, days, and weeks. The answers are there. You just need to know how to see, hear, feel, or recognize them. Some people ask for signs or interpret messages and answers in signs. A butterfly landing on you reassuring you that you're not alone and a loved one is nearby. A friend reaching out to you when you're feeling lonely or low. A song that randomly starts playing with lyrics that contain a message just for you. Literal signs on the road or outside that pop out to you with their resonating words. Messages and answers are all around, coming through all your senses.

Articulate Your Questions Clearly

What question are you seeking to answer, and why? To help get to the best answer to your question, it's important to first ensure you are asking the right question. Sometimes, the question we ask is not the root of what we are truly questioning. So, it is worthwhile to dig deeper and examine what it is you are even asking in the first place and why. Does the question get to the root of the issue at hand, the decision you are facing? For example, a question you may ask is, "Should I look for a new job?" In your mind, you may assume the new job is in the same industry or field you're currently in, but perhaps, with different responsibilities and compensation. However, in your gut, you know that you haven't felt satisfied in your career track for a while, and always wanted to do something completely different, in a more creative and artistic field, for instance, but have been afraid of failure and what others may think. In this case, the question can more accurately be reframed as, "Is staying in my current job and career path in my best interest?" or "Should I shift my career to a different field or industry?" or "Will I be successful in a different career path as an artist?" or "Will I be able to make just as much, if not more money in a career path as an artist?" Figure out what it truly is that you are asking, and why. Get to the core of your questioning. Get specific in your questioning so that there is no room for ambiguity or misinterpretation.

Next, it's critical to ensure that you are articulating your question properly. Think about each word you are using and consider whether your question could be misconstrued or misinterpreted if you articulated it to someone without any other context. Take the time to parse through your question, being direct wherever possible and precise in your language. A clear question will help get you a clearer answer. Ambiguous questions can be more difficult to receive answers for and may result in vague answers, or an answer that isn't wholly applicable. Get clear on why you are asking your question, and what you are asking. Break it into multiple questions if needed, and ensure you are not asking multiple questions in one. Continuing with the same example above, you may break your ask into multiple questions, such as, "Is staying in my current job in my best interest?". "Is staying in my current industry the most fulfilling career path I can take?", and "Will I be financially successful if I pursue a career as an artist?" Position your questions one at a time and wait to receive responses before proceeding to the next question.

Phrase your questions so that the answers are clearly either "yes" or "no". This is an important part of getting clearer answers. While it is possible to get answers to open-ended questions that don't have direct responses, it can be more difficult in the beginning. Asking "yes" or "no" questions will help you get a better feel for how you receive affirmative answers, versus how you receive negative answers. Get to the essence of your questioning, then break it down into direct, single, "yes" or "no" questions. Ask your questions one at a time and wait for an answer before moving onto the next. The clearer your questions are, the easier it will be to receive clearer answers.

Ask in Love Instead of Fear

Before you ask your question, I encourage you to be in a mental and physical space where you feel safe, calm, and grounded. If you are feeling anxious or fearful, your ego may step in and give you an answer reflecting that fear. Most people have not yet learned how to co-exist harmoniously with their ego and have instead allowed their ego to dominate. This ego may view anything unknown, different, or new as scary, and will do its best to try and protect you from potentially difficult or scary situations. If you ask your question while you're feeling anxious or in fear, your ego may step in to answer and point you toward the known versus the unknown. Often, this will lead to continuing down the same path you're already following, which may be out of fear, anxiety, and stress.

You can take yourself out of that fear mindset and energy when you ground and center yourself first before asking, allowing yourself to feel safe and calm as you put your question out there. When you ask your question, you are not looking for your ego to answer. You want to pay attention to the answers that come from a deeper place of wisdom. Ultimately, everyone wants to lead a happy, healthy, and peaceful life. Doing your best to feel open to that possibility, while also grounding and centering yourself before tuning into your heart center to ask your question, will help raise the energy around the question you're asking. That way, you'll receive an answer from your inner wisdom and intelligence that can lead to more love and less fear.

Receiving Your Answers

Recall from Chapter 2 that when the answers are right for you, you may feel calmer, lighter, or more expansive. When the answers aren't right for you, you may feel agitated, heavier, or more closed off. A "yes" response will correspond with feeling lighter, more relaxed, and open. A "no" response will correspond with feeling tighter, more constricted, or closed off. You may also receive your answers through different senses—seeing, hearing, knowing, or feeling. There isn't only one way to receive an answer from your intuition or inner wisdom. You can hear (clairaudient), see (clairvoyant), feel (clairsentient), or know (claircognizant) the answer. You may also receive your answers through more than one sense. Perhaps you feel and hear it, or see it and know it.

If you hear an answer, know that receiving the right answer for you is not about listening to any voice you may hear, as there may be different sources, including your ego or energies coming from a place of fear. Instead, tune into your feelings and ensure you're asking when you're feeling calm, present, and at peace. Be cautious of the answers that come back with judgement, fear, and criticism. It's best not to listen to them. Try to notice whether the answers come back loudly, with judgement, saying you "should" do this or that. Do your best to let those answers go. Rather, I want you to *sense* the right answers. Use all the senses that are available to you. Does the answer feel right?

Understand that the ego may respond to you, and it is often easier to hear the ego as it is loud and used to peppering you with criticism, worries, and judgement. On the other hand, your inner wisdom and intuition will speak to you calmly and clearly. What you're looking for is the answers that come to you calmly, directly, and with no judgement around them. These answers may come through softly, so, pay attention, but they are straight-forward and even in tone. Pay attention to the answers coming from a place of love, without judgement or fear. Your intuition and inner wisdom will answer clearly and calmly.

Your answers may come in signs, symbols, pictures, or words that you see in your mind, or in front of you as you go about your day. Your answers may be heard through words or phrases received internally, or literally hearing them in songs, videos, conversations, and so on. Set your intention, ask your question, and then be open and ready to see, hear, listen, and feel. Go out and notice what you notice. What jumps out at you? What resonates with you? And what does that mean? What is the deeper meaning behind these signs, symbols, images, words, and things that you see, hear, and feel? The universe will conspire to help you if you are clear in what you want and go after it.

I'll often get into the right energy and space to ask my questions by going for walks outside, which helps me clear my mind and connect to my body. I'll focus on my breathing for a while and then shift my focus to feeling my heart center as I walk in meditation. After some time, when I feel more settled, I'll ask my questions, one at a time, and see how my body feels or whether I get an answer. Place your awareness in your heart center, feel it open, breathe through that space, and ask. Oftentimes, I'll receive an answer before I even finish my question, and for me, many times, the answers are repetitious, especially in my writing. Everyone's experience is different, so tune in, and pay attention.

The Work – Ask From Your Heart

If you're still unsure of the best answer for you, try bringing the question into your heart center. Before you begin, it is helpful to be in a quiet space where you won't be disturbed. If you can, take a few minutes to breathe deeply, relax your body, and focus on your breath or heart center (the space in the center of your chest, behind your breastbone, and in front of your spine). If you have a preferred method of meditation and connecting within, take some time to do that first. When you feel relaxed and are focused in the present moment, set the intention to be open to connect to higher energies for your greatest and highest good, and then bring up the question internally and hold it in your heart center (keep your awareness on your heart center). Notice what you experience. You may get an answer right away, or feel nothing. Whatever you experience is fine. You may not receive an immediate answer, but continue to pay attention to signs and notice what you notice in the days to come. The universe will endeavour to answer and guide you, so, pay attention.

If you want to explore this further, you can also bring up each option or consideration for answers one at a time, after you pose the question. For each option, think of it, feel it, and imagine holding it in your heart center, or keep your focus on your heart center in your body as you think of the option. Notice and observe how each option feels to you, your body, and your heart center. Breathe deeply. Does it feel open and light, indicating an affirmative response? Or does it feel closed off and tight, indicating a negative response? What sensations or experiences do you notice, if any? Do you hear or see anything? What do you notice and feel? Try the same for the next option until you've gone through each one. You may want to take notes after each one, or write about the experience afterward.

Practice Practice Practice

Know that this work will take practice and time. Notice if the answers come loudly or quietly. How do the responses come through? How do they feel? Practice. Notice the difference in the answers you may receive when you are quiet, calm, and connected, versus the answers you receive when you are not connected to your heart center and are instead coming from a place of fear. Connecting to your intuition and inner wisdom is a skill that can be developed and strengthened over time and with practice, so, I encourage you to practice often.

Start practicing with simple questions you already know the answers to. This will give you a better feel for how your body may react, or how the authentic answers may come through. Try it with questions that have obvious "yes" or "no" answers for yourself. Remember that some people will feel them in their bodies, some will hear answers, while others will see them. Remember that your body and your gut feelings will help guide you.

When I started practicing, I asked myself easy questions to see how my answers felt and came through. For example, ask what your name is, and offer names that are not yours. See how you sense the answers. Use all your senses. When I started developing this skill of asking and learning how to listen and receive answers, I had some misunderstandings as I needed more practice, and that's perfectly fine. This is a skill that we all have, and one that has been underutilized or underdeveloped for most people. So, I encourage you to practice with simple questions where you already know the obvious answers, and do your best to get out of your head and into your heart. You can and will build this skill up, just like exercising a muscle, with practice, practice, practice.

Understanding Answers

When you ask a question and receive an answer, know that it doesn't mean you must choose to run with or act on that answer. It is still your choice as to what you do next, so, take your time to sit with it and feel it out if you need to. Also, know that answers are not absolute. They are not the final and only answer. It simply may be the best answer for you in the given situation and time. As time passes and circumstances change, the answer to your question may also change. Receiving answers is not about predicting the future and exact details. Instead, it is feeling the best choice or path for you to take at that time. You are the best guide for yourself. Do not be quick to allow others to make decisions for you. Own your free will, and understand that the purpose of turning inward to get the best answer for yourself is not to follow those answers blindly, but rather to know that you can ask for guidance and connect to your intuition. Ultimately, you are in charge of your life, and you always have a choice. The choices you make and the answers you choose need to resonate with you. It has to feel right for you, and it has to be right for you, which is something only you can decide.

Journal to Your Answers

A practice I like to use often is journaling to my answers. I'll center and connect first with my meditation practice, and then open my journal and write my question. Then, I'll tune into what comes through. For some people, it may be easier to get answers through your writing and when in the flow. This can include drawing or scribbling to help get the energy moving. There are many ways to get into the flow. My daily practice involves going to my yoga mat for an intuitive energy move-ment practice. Sometimes, this looks like yoga, and other times it looks like tai chi or martial arts. At times, it is a mix of all three, and it usually ends in a sitting meditation. Your way of getting into the flow may look different. Do what makes you feel at peace, calm, grounded, and connected. After my intui-tive energy movement practice, I pick up my journal, sit down, and write. I turn inwards and ask, "What does my soul want to tell me today?" Then, I wait to receive an answer. If I have specific questions, I write them down as I ask and then wait for an answer, which I often get through feeling, knowing, and hearing. For me, writing out questions makes it easier to get answers, and once I'm writing, the messages and answers flow, one after another.

Like how I asked my soul that question, you can ask your question to anyone you wish, such as a guide, angel, ances-tor, loved one who has passed, divine source, god, and so on. Remember to remain at your heart center when asking. When I first started this practice and wasn't as familiar with the energies and intuition I was tuning into, I ensured to preface my questions with the phrase that I'm asking for answers and messages for my greatest and highest good. As you start out, it may be unclear as to how to interpret the answers that do come in, so, continue to practice, doing The Work and exercises, and it'll get easier to receive the answers over time.

Tips:

- Get clear on what your question is truly about. Take time to examine your question. Does it get to the heart of what you're asking and want to know? To help get clearer answers, be specific with your questions, and frame them into "yes" or "no" questions, breaking them down into multiple questions if needed.
- Ensure your questions are precisely and clearly worded. Phrase your question in a way that there is no room for misinterpretation. Choose your words carefully. Answers that are in your best interest are direct and non-judgemental; however, if your question isn't worded clearly, you may not get the answers that are truly best for you.
- Ask your question when you are feeling calm, grounded, and centered. The more you can feel light, connected, and at peace with asking your question, the better.
- Try writing out your questions in your journal and use all your senses to receive the answers.
- You may choose to direct your questions to those you feel connected to, or feel are here for your greatest and

highest good (i.e., your soul or higher self, a deceased loved one, the universe, divine, god, angels, guides, etc.).

- Sit with your answers. How do they feel? How does your body feel? Does the answer resonate with you? Sometimes, you may get an answer and instinctively know that it's right. Other times, you may get an answer that you weren't expecting, and if you're feeling unsure, just be with the answer. If the answer is seemingly coming out of left field, you don't have to have blind faith and just leap. You can also choose to just be with it and see if your feelings change over time. Some people *know* that the answers they receive are for their highest interest, so, they will do it, even if it seems odd, and find that they were led down an unexpected path that yielded amazing experiences. You need to do what's right for you, even when you receive an answer. It's your choice whether you wish to act on that answer or not.

- Don't be afraid of change. Sometimes, the answers may feel right, but you're afraid that the path won't be easy, assuming that it may result in others being angry with you, relationships ending, or taking a big risk. Change need not be feared. Making assumptions does not help. The greater the challenge, the more it will bring you. It may open the way for new experiences and relationships that you wouldn't have had space for otherwise, if you stayed on the safe path. Don't be afraid to make decisions that are right for you.

The Work – Manifestation Exercise

We are all connected—whether we realize it or not—to the beings, space, world, and energies around us. In this invisible space of connection, you can ask your questions and receive answers. There is a world of possibilities in your life, and a key step in getting what you want is to ask, to put it out there into the universe, and to declare your intention. To help practice your asking and receiving abilities, and to demonstrate to yourself their power, you can try this manifestation exercise. This is the same exercise I did to get multiple, free, delectable Japanese meals. Try not to be disappointed if you feel like it didn't work for you. Keep doing The Work in this book to help you get your message out there, and to help you better receive and see the answers.

- Take a few deep breaths, turning your attention inward. Feel calm and relaxed.
- Now, recall what it is you would like to manifest. What is it? What does it look like? What would it feel like to have it? Picture it, see it, and feel it. Use all your senses and vivid imagination. Feel gratitude for it.
- Now, let go. Let go of your ask. If you are constantly thinking about why you haven't received something yet, the message and energy you're sending out is one of lack instead of gratitude. Once you made your ask, felt what it would be like to have it, expressed and felt gratitude for it, let it go. You're done.

- For smaller requests, you can play around with putting a timeline against it. For larger requests, know that it may take time for things to line up, so, be patient. Wait and see.
- Start working toward the manifestation to help it come to fruition. This is not about making blind wishes and sitting back without putting in any human effort. The ask you put out there, along with the work you put into bringing about the manifestation, work together.
- If you can, live your life as if you already have what you want, as this will help it come more easily. How would you feel if your manifestation came true? Start feeling that way as you go about your life.

CHAPTER 7

Dream Interpretation

*Trust the dreams, for in them is
hidden the gate to eternity.*
Kahlil Gibran, *The Prophet*

I WAS COMING AROUND to the decision to have surgery for the colon cancer diagnosis, but I wasn't sure which surgeon to go with. Dr. S, the surgical oncologist assigned to me, worked at the same hospital as my sister-in-law, often working together in the same operating room. She trusted him and told me I was in good hands. I felt like everything was happening very quickly, and I needed time for myself to digest and process everything. I wanted to take time to ask questions, do my own research, advocate for myself, and most importantly, look inward and feel comfortable with any decision I made. From my research, I found that the top-rated surgical oncologist in the city was at a nearby hospital. So, I made an appointment to see him for a second opinion. I also got a reference from my family doctor for another surgeon at the same hospital where I gave birth to my daughter. I was fortunate to have many qualified options. As I waited for my appointment with the top-rated surgeon, I got my questions ready, armed with the knowledge I had gathered to advocate for myself. In our appointment, I ran through my list of questions, and in the end, he agreed with the treatment that Dr. S had recommended. Moreover, he told me that he and Dr. S were acquaintances, and vouched for his skills, while suggesting it would be best to stay with Dr. S. In fact, they both told me they would choose each other to perform the surgery I was going to undertake if they ever needed it.

While I was waiting for my appointment with the third surgeon, I intuitively decided to turn to my dreams for answers. The practice was relatively new for me, having heard about it and trying it a couple of times before without any memorable results. As I faced the critical life decisions associated with the diagnosis, I became more open to trying different things that could provide guidance and reassurance. Before going to sleep, I wrote my questions in my journal. For three nights in a row, I asked, "Who do I go with for surgery?" or "Which doctor should I book with?" The first night, I recalled a dream where the actor, Henry Winkler, appeared, looked me in the eyes, and said, "Take things slowly." I didn't have a prior connection or particular affinity for him. In fact, I had to look him up to confirm his name, which felt very random and interesting. Looking back, I can now see that perhaps the lack of connection to him signalled the advice from an objective third party. The second night after I wrote the same question in my journal, I could not recall any dreams when I awoke. On the third night, I had a dream and wrote it in my journal, describing how I had decided to grow green pea plants in the house, and was searching for three separate planters to grow them in. I was in a home hardware store, in the aisle with planters, looking at different kinds of containers and trying to decide which one to choose. There were hammered copper planters, clay planters, ceramic planters, and more, all in different shapes and colours, and there I was, just looking at the aisle, pondering which to choose. Then, I woke up. In my journal, I wrote, "My interpretation is that the three doctors, like the different planters, will do the same job. They just look different, so, I just have to choose one." When I recalled my dream that morning, I realized that my dream was telling me that it didn't matter whether I chose the hammered copper, clay, or ceramic planter. The pea plants would all grow equally well in them. I realized that the message I got from my dream was the same. I wrote in my journal that I was leaning toward staying with the doctor that had been assigned to me. It wasn't just interpreting the dream that helped me; it was checking in with myself to see what felt right. The next day, I made the decision to tell my doctor that I would move forward with surgery and cancelled my consultation appointment with the third surgeon. I had made my decision.

The Meaning Behind Dreams

The dreams you experience may feel weird, random, intense, and very different from your earthly life. Your dreams are not confined by the time and space paradigms of your waking reality, so, they can be confusing to understand or make meaning of. As a result, many people will simply dismiss them as inconsequential and meaningless. Some may acknowledge them as just our brains sorting through experiences from our lives that have occurred, while others feel and know that our dreams are more. They are a portal to the unseen world with wisdom and intelligence that we can experience and access more easily when we are asleep. Your dreams are experiences you have in an alternate state, where you may be more receptive to guidance than in your day-to-day reality. They hold messages and guidance you can receive if you know how to interpret and listen to them.

As I started writing this chapter about dream interpretations, I took the opportunity to explore my dreams even more. I signed up for a dream course with Robert Moss, a dream teacher who helped me uncover a new depth in my dream interpretations. I fully align with his approach and words, in which he states, "Dreaming isn't just what happens during sleep; dreaming is waking up to sources of guidance, healing and creativity beyond the reach of the everyday mind."[22] In one of the guided sessions during his course, I connected with ancestors, feeling a sensation in the upper left side of my head. They shared with me a message that everything in dreams have a meaning and encouraged me to dig deeper. Looking back at the planter dream two and a half years later with this new awareness, I realized that the planters did not simply symbolize each doctor as I had initially interpreted, but instead, a choice I could make to hold space for myself to grow new roots, stretch higher, and produce seeds for further growth. Just as the planters provide space and a container for the pea plants to grow in, moving forward with my treatment allowed me to slow down and hold space for myself in the sense that I took time off work to be still, rest, and heal. Just as plants grow roots, holding that space for myself allowed me to build a stronger foundation for myself. Just as plants grow taller, stretching higher toward the sun, the roots and space allowed me to rise and ascend in my life, shedding the parts of me that were heavy and weighing me down. Just as the pea plants produce seeds, I was able to collect the knowledge and wisdom gained from taking space, rooting deeply, and growing taller as a being, to be able to share with others so that they may also grow deeper, taller, and further. Remembering the message that everything in a dream has a meaning, I looked up pea plants and learned that pea plants self-pollinate, meaning they are not dependent on another to fertilize them. Choosing to grow pea plants in my dream was symbolic insofar as I was choosing to step into my own growth, not looking for outside validation to determine my ability to thrive.

Dreams have been analyzed and studied for centuries. While the dreams may not be "real" in our waking lives, the emotions are, and they reveal what may be hidden to us in our realities. Dreams help us process emotions that may be suppressed or not fully expressed. In a study called *The Science Behind Dreaming*, author, Sander van Der Linder, described how dreaming enables us to unconsciously process emotions, "This way, the emotion itself is no longer active. This mechanism fulfils an important role because when we don't process our emotions, especially negative ones, this increases personal worry and anxiety. In fact, severe REM sleep-deprivation (most dreaming and our most intense dreams occur during the REM stage) is increasingly correlated to the development of mental disorders. In short, dreams help regulate traffic on that fragile bridge which connects our experiences with our emotions and memories."[23]

Sigmund Freud wrote, "The interpretation of dreams is the royal road to a knowledge of the unconscious activities of the mind." He understood and espoused that every dream was meaningful, and that the interpretation of them were personal. A dream dictionary definition found in a book or online cannot solely tell you the absolute meaning of an object or symbol in a dream, as these interpretations and connotations are personal, and thus, need to resonate with the dreamer to hold truth in the meaning behind them. Over the years, there have been numerous studies on dreams, with a commonly held notion that dreams help you process emotions and experiences. Many people have recurring dreams of traumatic experiences and seek a way to end these dreams. I've found that once I was able to acknowledge and process these dreams, they dissipated. In other words, once I understood why I was having those dreams and worked on letting go of whatever emotions I was holding onto—namely fear—the recurring dreams ceased.

For years after I graduated from university, I had a recurring dream that it was my final exam for finance class, and I had neglected to study, leaving me feeling panicked as I faced the test wondering why I never studied. This particular class was one I found very difficult and was also one I needed to graduate in my chosen degree. I remember thinking that if I didn't pass, I wouldn't be able to graduate with my class, and everyone would know I was a failure. Furthermore, I envisioned how that failure would trickle into my GPA, subsequent inability to pursue an MBA, and mar me from being able to land a successful job and career. All these weren't necessarily true, but I felt fear as if they were. When I awoke, I told myself I was safe, I passed, and I was fine, over and over again.

Dreams reveal so much more than most of us realize. They can help us sort through situations and guide us to the right next steps. In our everyday lives, many of us have our ego, ongoing mind chatter, and thoughts clouding our ability to receive and recognize the best answers for ourselves. When you are physically asleep, you are in a different state of mind or dimension, often more receptive of messages that may be hard to see or hear when you're awake. It will take some practice, but you can receive wisdom and guidance from your dreams if you know how to listen and interpret them. Luckily, you are your own best dream guide and interpreter. While you may use other resources like this book, talking to others, or gathering information online to help understand some of the hidden meanings behind your dreams, you are ultimately best equipped to interpret your own dreams and to glean the guidance being given. That is because you'll know your interpretation is on track when it feels rights, and when it resonates. I encourage you to start practicing dream interpretation as another avenue to get to the best answers for you.

The Work – Dream Interpretation

To start, it is important to put your intention out there, including your question. Choose something to write or record your dreams, experiences, and interpretations in. It can be your journal, a separate dream notebook, your phone, laptop, or even a voice recorder. Do this exercise before you go to sleep.

1. Take some time to get comfortable, and then close your eyes and turn your attention inward. Focus on your breathing for a few moments, noticing your breath as it comes in and out of your body. Then, turn your attention to your heart center. This is the space in the center of your chest, inside your body, behind your sternum/breastbone, and in front of your spine. Hold your awareness in your heart center for a few breaths.

2. Now, bring forward the question that you are seeking guidance on. You are setting your intention when you do this, putting forward the request or stating the subject that you wish to focus on, and learning more about. Hold that question in your heart center, doing your best to keep this space open. Feel free to repeat the question while you are keeping your awareness on the space in your heart center. Add in anything else that may feel right for you, like visualizing the words, holding a crystal, or continuing to focus on your breath. Then, write your question in your journal. Remember, be clear and articulate in your question so that there isn't any room for misinterpretation. Ask one question at a time. If it's an area you're seeking guidance on and don't necessarily have a specific question for, you can state your intention on that subject. For example, statements regarding your career may look like the following, "I am asking to receive guidance about my career,

in my best interest, and for my highest and greatest good."

3. For any question or intention that you bring forward, add that you are asking for answers or guidance "in your best interests and for your highest and greatest good." Feel it and clearly state that intention.

4. Now, let go of the question. Release it. Relax, and go to bed. It's best not to have an alarm set so that you're not startled awake in the morning, which may cause you to forget your dream experience. If you can, allow yourself to slowly come out of sleep so you can more easily retain the experience you had in your dream state.

5. If you wake up in the middle of the night, take some time to recollect any dream experiences you had in your sleep, and record them if you wish. Then, restate your intention or question before settling back into sleep.

6. When you wake up in the morning, take some time to be still. Don't reach for your phone or get out of bed right away. Be still, and then take your time to remember and recall your dreams, if any, that you had. How do you feel about the experience and how did you feel while in the experience? Even if you can't recall any dreams, notice how you feel when you first wake up. Then, write or record the details, your experience, and feelings. Consider the following:

   • What happened in the dream? What details and events do you remember?

- How do you feel about the dream and the experience? How did you feel in the dream? How do you feel recollecting the dream?
- How may this relate to your life?
- What do you feel this dream is reflecting?
- What do you feel the dream is telling you?

Dream interpretations are personal, and they are not necessarily straightforward. Metaphors for your life experiences and answers are likely to be found in your seemingly random dream recollections, and it is up to you to sift through, examine the dream, and feel what it means. When discovering answers in your dreams, you may find that your dream experiences don't often give literal answers (although they can at times). Answers are often metaphorical, where the dreams are asking you to *dig a little deeper* and explore new ways of thinking and being. In some ways, it reminds me of high school English classes, where we would discuss the meaning, analogies, and metaphors behind an author's words. Many of the messages in the stories were obvious or clear with a little research and introspection; however, for others, I sometimes question the interpretations given by the teacher. Some of them felt like a stretch to me, and I remember feeling doubtful that they could know the absolute truth behind the words, often wondering, *How do you know what this author meant or felt?* I didn't fully buy into the narrative that my English teacher, with no worldly connection to the author, could have known what they truly meant or felt in the depths of their being. When applied to your dream interpretations, the same thing is true—

only you know how you feel. They are your dreams, and you are your own best interpreter. When you start examining your dreams, you'll know when the meaning, messages, and signs you've uncovered are right because you'll feel them. They will resonate.

That said, I feel it can be helpful to look up aspects of your dream in a dream dictionary, book, or online to better understand or spark what some of the experiences in your dream are alluding to. The same can be said for getting feedback on your dream experiences from others. Keep what resonates and leave what doesn't. When examining your dreams, also take into consideration what is happening in your life, what issues you're dealing with, and how you've been feeling. For example, I had a dream where I recall opening my fridge, but noticing that the fridge and freezer below were full of loaves of bread, each a different brand and type. I wondered, *Where did all this bread come from?* After I awoke from my dream, I looked up the meaning of bread in a dream dictionary and found that it represented abundance and nourishment. I resonated with the interpretation that I would always have more than enough to eat, to live, and to prosper. Growing up, I had a mindset that I had to work hard and succeed for myself out of fear I wouldn't have enough money and there would be no one to depend on. Part of my personal journey has been understanding and accepting that it doesn't have to be that hard, that I don't have to be *doing* things all the time, and I can still receive and have abundance. That I am not alone, and don't have to do everything by myself and for myself. A few months prior to this dream, I was at a meditation retreat, and during a random conversation with someone I'd just met, he shared that his accountant told him, "You better start spending your money because you're never going to run out." As soon as those words exited his mouth, they reverberated and echoed in my mind, loudly, like someone was yelling them at me, telling me this message was for me, too. When I had the dream about the bread, I recalled this incident, and felt it was further validation of this message. Stepping back, I realize that this dream also came during a phase in my life where I had recently quit my corporate job and was taking time to slow down and heal. As I did this inner work, I was also figuring out what my next career steps would be. During this time, I slowly re-integrated and added activities that I truly loved, including teaching yoga and meditation. My passion has always been helping others live happier and healthier lives; however, I had always done those activities on the side through part-time yoga teaching, volunteer work, and mentoring. I had convinced myself that I wouldn't be able to have the level of financial and career success I wanted if I worked in health and wellness full-time. Now I recognize that was a limiting belief, and the bread in my dream was telling me that I can do what I love and be abundant. That I will never run out of nourishment and wealth. Perhaps even as I nourished others with this personal work, I would receive abundance and nourishment in return. I interpreted the fact that there were different brands and types of bread in the dream to indicate that my abundance and wealth would come from different sources and areas.

Tips:

Dream interpretations take time and practice, so, try not to feel frustrated if it doesn't come easily at first. There have been many times after I wake up and recollect a dream where I initially think, *I have no idea what this means. It seems completely vague and random.* However, once I *dig deeper*, sit with the dream experiences, examine how I felt and feel, and consider what it could relate to in my life, I often come to interpretations that afterward feel obvious to me. Some tools to aid you with your dream recollection and interpretations are as follows:

- Ask your higher self or soul to help you remember your dreams. You can ask this anytime, including when you first wake up, and before you go to bed.
- Replay your dreams in your mind as you start to gently awaken. I like to recall my dream while laying still in bed, replaying it as I have found it helps me remember it before I write it down later in the day. Sometimes, I talk with my husband about our respective dreams. I'll tell him about mine, and I'll ask him about his.
- If you don't recall any of your dreams when you wake up, notice how you feel. The dream experiences can leave you with feelings that you can work with in your waking life.
- Discuss your dreams with a trusted partner, friend, or group who is also interested in dream interpretations. Robert Moss has outlined a way to share dreams with others that I've found helpful. He suggests to i) give

your dream a title, ii) write how you felt during and after the dream, iii) consider whether this could happen in real life, the future, or the past, and iv) consider what your action plan would be. When you find your group or partner to share dreams with, share with them a summary of the dream, how you felt, and what you feel it may mean or symbolize, and then listen to their comments and feedback. If you're participating in discussion regarding other people's dreams, as well, it's important that you don't tell others what you think their dream means, but simply share how you would approach it if it were your dream experience. This allows you to share helpful feedback rather than prescriptive. Remember that you are your own best dream interpreter, so, take what resonates, and leave the rest. Be mindful of this when providing feedback, as well as receiving it.

- Dream re-entry. I also learned the valuable exercise of dream re-entry from Robert Moss. This is an activity in which you go back into your dreams through a meditation experience to continue with the dream journey and learn more. I've outlined the way that I do this on my own in The Work below.

The Work – Dream Re-entry

To help better understand a particular dream and the messages within it, I may go back into the dream experience with a dream re-entry. This can be helpful when I am unsure of the interpretation, and I want to go back to experience and feel more. Have your dream in mind that you want to explore deeper when you start your dream re-entry. You can choose to have soft music playing in the background if you wish. If you do play music, you may find meditation music, nature sounds, or solfeggio frequencies for your third eye chakra helpful.

- Get into a comfortable meditation position seated or laying down, with a tall neck and spine, relaxing your shoulders and chest.
- Close your eyes and relax your body even more. If you prefer not to close your eyes, look down towards your nose in a soft gaze.
- Turn your attention inward to your breathing, just noticing your inhales and exhales for a few breaths. Then, take a few slower and deeper breaths in and out of your nose.
- Feel your heart center, turning your awareness to the space in the center of your chest, inside your body. Try to soften this space. Feel it relax and open.
- Keeping your heart center open, let go of anything in your mind, doing your best to empty it, and keep your awareness on your open heart center. Bring your mind back to opening and softening your heart center anytime it wanders away. Empty your mind, open your heart, and just feel.
- Now, bring in the intention to re-enter your chosen dream experience. Internally or out loud, state your

intention to return to your dream to learn and experience more. You may also bring in the intention to speak with a specific character from your dream experience. Remember to include the intention "to connect for your highest and greatest good" while you feel that in your heart center.

- Bring yourself back to your dream, start to recollect, and then let go, allowing the experience to take you. You may feel that you're just imagining things, and that is perfectly fine. Ask questions or start a dialogue with a particular character. Do your best not to stress or feel anxious if you find it difficult to re-enter your dreams. Simply wait, feel your heart center open, and keep the intention to re-enter your dream experience.
- When you feel you are finished, open your eyes, and take some time to recollect what occurred, how you felt, how you currently feel, writing or recording your experiences as you go.

Exploring your dreams is a fertile world for guidance, messages, lessons, and support. While this practice may be more "out there" than The Work in previous chapters, I have no doubt these strategies can help lead you to your best answers.

CHAPTER 8

Love is the Answer

Let love be your guide.

YEARS AGO, NOT long after my first heartbreak, I was in a new relationship with someone who was kind-hearted and treated me better than I knew possible at the time. He also happened to be half-Jamaican and half-Chinese, and for my immigrant Chinese mom who had heard repeatedly over the years from my father that he would disown his kids if we ever partnered with someone who wasn't Chinese, it was difficult to accept. My mother is very loving and kind-hearted, as well as relatively submissive to my father, which was the norm for all moms I knew then, as they were raised within a traditional, misogynistic culture and society. I knew that it didn't matter that my kind-hearted boyfriend was half-Chinese; it wouldn't be enough for them, and my relationship would cause major issues, having known of other family members being disowned for loving someone outside our race. Despite this, my mother and I were close, and I couldn't lie to her about my new relationship (it was a secret from my father).

We were out having pho together at one of our favourite restaurants one day and she questioned why I was with my then current boyfriend instead of someone like my ex-boyfriend, a Chinese Canadian. I told her that my previous boyfriend didn't treat me well in the end, and my eyes burned with tears as I exclaimed that I couldn't believe she would want me to be with someone who treated me poorly instead of with someone who treated me with kindness just because of their race. I asked her if she would want her daughter, me, to have the kind of marriage that she had, and to be treated in the same way by her husband, and she didn't answer. "Why would you want your daughter to be with someone of the same race if it wasn't a kind, loving relationship?" I pushed. She sat there looking down at her food in silence, her absence of words speaking volumes. I couldn't bring myself to talk to her for a while after that.

Finally, one day, she came to me and apologized. She told me that since our last conversation, she hadn't been able to sleep well, and realized that she had been racist and wrong. The situation had forced her to examine her actions and words in a new light. Assuring me that it didn't matter who I chose to be with and that she just wanted me to be happy, she asked for my forgiveness, which I readily gave. In the end, my mother was able to look past her fear of the unknown and how my relationship would be perceived by others, ultimately trusting in love to come to her best answer.

Love. This is the last step outlined in *The Answer*; however, it is the most powerful when pervasive throughout your journey. I could fill a whole book on love and how it will lead you to your best answers and life. Love is much more than a four-letter word. There is so much that this simple word encompasses—more than many of us first think of when we hear the word "love." It extends beyond romance, family, and friendship. It is not limited to the world of humans and animals. You can feel love, speak love, hear love, taste love, and see love. In a broad sense, love can be a spectrum of emotions, including but not limited to kindness, compassion, gratitude, playfulness, forgiveness, empathy, and more. It is what we feel when we're happy, laughing, grateful, and sharing. Love is a currency, a connection, and an exchange, where the more we give, the more we get. Love is beauty, and beauty is everywhere. It is no mistake that love is the answer in many fairy tales and stories. It can truly set us free, and it begins with loving ourselves. If you find it difficult to make decisions or are often conflicted about the choices in your life, it is likely you are lacking in love for yourself. Often, we forget to share love with the person in our life that needs it the most from us: ourselves. Being loving to yourself is a gateway to your best life and the choices to take to get there.

Loving yourself starts with being kind. It can be so easy to criticize and put yourself down, to minimize who you are and the space you take. On the flip side, when you do something well, it can be harder to recognize and acknowledge. However, it wasn't always this way. Babies happily clap at their own accomplishments of stacking blocks or taking their first steps, cheered on by their loved ones. They don't criticize themselves when they stumble on their steps or trip over their feet; they just get up and keep going. Somewhere along the way in life, you started to slow yourself down with judgment and fear, worrying about and fearing the next step. Now, most of us tend to focus more on what went wrong, or what more we should have done, and gloss over what we accomplished and did well. However, we all deserve as much praise and recognition as we did when we were babies—new to this earthly world—because we're still figuring our way through life. The learning never ends. If we were all perfect, we wouldn't be human beings. There is nothing you have done to make you deserve any less. Everyone has something to learn, and focusing on your problems, what you lack, cannot or did not do, does not help; it only detracts.

Focusing on the solution and taking a moment or space to celebrate, recognize, or pat yourself on the back for what you did or do helps. This does not make you conceited or self-centered; rather, it makes you more loving to yourself. Do you notice that it is often easier to be loving, kind, and considerate to others, yet difficult to treat yourself with the same respect? You deserve more—we all do. It doesn't matter how much you already have to be grateful for in your life—the privilege, money, success, family, home, or relationships you have don't preclude you from having more. There is a false scarcity mindset that if someone is successful or has something, someone else won't. That is only true if we make it that way. In reality, there is more than enough for everyone. There is always more that you can gain to be appreciative of, and not everything is material. The most valuable is intangible: wisdom, knowledge, a sense of security, confidence, and feeling loved.

A simple yet often overlooked truth is that the relationship we have with ourselves is the most important one we have, and it has a profound impact on our life, as well as every single relationship and interaction we have during our time here on earth. Treat yourself with kindness and respect, and you'll have that mirrored in your life. Treat yourself with criticism and judgement, and you'll also project that onto others, only inviting more of the same into your own life. What kind of life do you want to live? A life full of love begins with loving yourself. So, start now. If you take one thing away from this book, I would be happy if it was to love yourself, fully and unconditionally. To do your best at this every day, and if you do, the changes that will unfold in your life will be nothing short of magical. Your answers will appear.

Loving yourself means treating yourself with respect, kindness, consideration, generosity, and without criticism, judgement, or expectations. It may sound like a tall order, but these changes can happen gradually until they feel more natural and become embedded into your life and relationship with yourself. Not internally berating yourself for something "wrong" that you said. Not calling yourself names or putting yourself down, even in a joking manner. Allowing yourself to breathe, to be, to enjoy time, space, and activities that are just for you. Self-care, in whatever way that feels right for you. That may look like taking a long bath with relaxing music, dancing in your room, writing in a journal, or breathing deeply and intentionally every day as you step outside for a walk. When you love yourself unconditionally, your answers will unfold and become clearer. The path to choose is always the path of love, and that is where your best answers lay.

Stay Heart Centered

You can access your best answers to almost any of your questions with love. Sounds simple, but it takes work to put into action. However, once you've started doing The Work, it'll get easier, and you'll be rewarded in ways you never even thought possible.

The answers and guidance that are for your greatest good can be accessed by staying heart centered. This means feeling from the heart, instead of thinking from the brain. When you are faced with a decision and are unsure, bring that question into your heart center. Hold it there, feel that space, and allow the best answer for you to surface. It may take practice to stay heart centered, so don't feel discouraged if it's difficult, or if you don't receive an answer right away. Continue connecting to your heart center, as this is where you connect to your soul's wisdom, love, and guidance. Your answers will come when the time is right.

The Work – Role Play

Imagine that someone you love dearly—and ideally, unconditionally—has come to you for advice. This is a person whom you want nothing but the best for, like your child, niece, nephew, or best friend. They briefly describe to you an issue they are having, and the decision they are wrestling with. It all sounds familiar because I want you to imagine it is the same situation as your own—the same circumstances and questions.

If that loved one came to you with the same burning question you have for yourself, what advice would you give? What would you say? What is it that you hope they would do next? Take a moment to consider these questions. Now, consider why you're unsure what to do next with the same question for yourself.

When we step back and examine someone else's issues, we can look at them without the added layers of complexities we place on our own. Did it feel a lot easier for you to give someone else advice on the same question you're dealing with versus answering it for yourself? Perhaps you've always known, deep down, the best answer, but it's not an easy answer. When you step back into your own perspective, you cloud the issue with layers of complexities, ifs and buts, and tell yourself it's not that simple, but it is. Perhaps you're scared. The answer makes you uncomfortable, brings up anxieties or fears, and takes you into unknown territory. When we take away the fear, worries, and conditions we place on ourselves and look only with the lens of love, the answers become much clearer. If you know the right answer for yourself but aren't ready to make it yet, how do you get there? With love. Love for yourself. By being patient, kind, and loving to yourself. By giving yourself space. Not space to run away from the issue, but instead to be with and face the issue in your own time and terms, until you're ready for the next step.

A journey of a thousand miles
starts beneath one's feet.

Lao Tzu, *Tao Te Ching*

The Next Step is Enough

You don't always need to figure out your final answer—just the next step. When you fixate on making the "right" answer or choice, you may become frozen, fearful of making the wrong choice, and end up stagnant. Sometimes a big decision, or the perceived consequences of that choice, can feel insurmountable. You may have a feeling of what's best for you; however, you also know that it will mean facing a difficult or uncomfortable challenge, and thus, you've stayed put for so long. You may feel like you don't even know where or how to start. But you can do this. Just focus on the next small step, that's it. Taking a step can encompass many things, a thought, feeling, intention, small, medium, or big action, and everything in between. Not all your steps need to be huge leaps of faith, as that's not how we walk through life. Take one step at a time. The momentum of those steps will fuel you when you arrive at those leaps of faith, and by that point, they won't feel as daunting. Instead, there will be a knowing that it is the right answer for you, the right next step. All the small steps, actions, and choices you make toward that decision will add up, and when you turn around one day, you will be in awe of how far you've come. Trust that taking one step at a time, no matter how small, will bring you closer to your answer. Just making the next step is enough. You don't always have to know where exactly you'll end up.

Be Where You Are

Be present with your steps, instead of worrying about what's ten steps ahead, or re-living perceived missteps behind you. Be where you are. Feel your steps. Be present with them. After all, your answer is only one of many choices in your life journey— not the be all and end all—as life is a compilation of all the choices you make. If you are always looking ahead to where you might be going or behind to where you've come from, you won't be able to fully experience where you are now. Everything you do in life is a choice, ranging from seemingly benign and simple choices—like getting out of bed in the morning, and brushing your teeth—to weightier choices like accepting a job, moving into a new home, or taking the next step in a relationship. Life is a series of choices.

When you don't know the best answer to your question, or you're not ready to make that choice yet, that's okay. Just be where you are. How does it feel? If you feel comfortable and satisfied to stay where you are, then that's great. Be fully there with all your senses and enjoy. If you, however, feel that it's time for a change, focus on taking that next step. While you're wrestling with figuring out what you want, sometimes it's easier to know what you don't want, and the next step is simply away from that. For example, maybe you're in a career that you know isn't right for you anymore and feel in your core that it's time to do something else, but you're not sure what that is or what it'll look like. You don't have to know exactly what the next job will be, you just have to take the next step, however small or big that may be. That could look like talking to a trusted friend, mentor,

LOVE IS THE ANSWER

or colleague about how you're feeling, or signing up for a course you're interested in. It could mean taking some vacation time to give yourself space and time to process how you're feeling and what you want to do next. It could be volunteering in an area of interest, or even starting a part-time business that excites you. It may be quitting your job to give yourself time and space to decompress, and then figuring out what you want to do next.

What you do next doesn't have to be viewed as a replacement, an equal, or even a better job. It is not about leaving one job for another, rather understanding that you are making a choice to leave something that is no longer right for you or has run its course. Sometimes, jumping from one thing to the next isn't the right answer. After all, a job doesn't define you. It is something you do, not who you are (although many people conflate the two). You are not what you do, and just because you are no longer "your job title", it doesn't mean you are no longer you. At times, what you need most is not to jump into the next thing, be it a job, relationship, or city, but time to just be. Space to breathe, relax, and allow yourself to feel. Spending time alone, taking time off work, prioritizing time for what you enjoy, going on vacation, quitting your job, or taking a few minutes to breathe mindfully all help give you time and space to get to the next best step and maybe the next best answer.

Enjoy each step. You don't always have to have it all figured out. As humans, it is hard for us to let go and just trust that the steps we take in life will lead us to where we think we want to be. Can you trust that being in the present, and taking the best steps for yourself, will lead you to where you need to be? Trust that your steps will lead you to something bigger than you

170

knew possible. You don't always need to know exactly where it will lead you, just go where it feels right. What is important to remember is that it's always about the now. So, try not to get ahead of yourself and beyond the next step. Your path doesn't end with the next decision you make, no matter how significant it may seem. There are more decisions to make after that, and more steps to take. What's important is that you're headed in the right direction. Your life on earth is a journey, not a destination. Each decision you make is another step on that journey. Sometimes, as humans, we get so wrapped up in the world we've immersed ourselves into that we forget that. We think that the next job, relationship, or place will solve our issues, and everything will be better. But that only changes your surroundings; it doesn't change you within. The journey to your best answers is a journey within.

Love Yourself

Loving yourself means giving yourself the space, time, consideration, and patience for the best answers. It is allowing yourself to just be. When you focus on being kind to yourself, practice self-care, do The Work and take time to enjoy just being you, your best answers will inevitably come. The right next step for you will become obvious, and harder to ignore. The more you love yourself, the more you will naturally allow your life to unfold in a way that's best for you. You don't always need to know the best answer, just the next best step on your journey. That next step will lead you to the next, and the next, and the ones that follow. Step toward love and away from fear, and know that your best answers will be in that direction.

The best answers to almost any question can be found with love. When you choose love instead of fear, you invite more love back to you. When you make choices out of fear, you invite more fear back to you. However, many of us choose fear because it feels easier or even more comfortable. It is a familiar choice. But you've been down that road and know how it feels in the end. Be fearless and choose your answers with love. Treat yourself with love, choose the answer or next step that you'd want someone you love unconditionally to choose if they were in your shoes. When you notice your thoughts veering into fear, let them go without any judgement, and choose loving thoughts instead. If choosing loving thoughts is too much of a stretch, you can simply be in the present, or choose neutral, fact-based thoughts. Fear perpetuates fear. Love perpetuates love. Practice feeling love as you go about your daily activities and work. Every moment of every day you have a choice. You can choose to walk around with love in your heart, or with fear and anger. Your choices invite more of the same. Choose wisely.

Love your body, your mind, your soul, and your whole self. No one is perfect. We're here to experience, fail, learn, grow, and love. You don't need to love your past negative experiences, as that may be challenging, but you can get to a place where you accept them, recognize the lessons within, and are grateful for the lessons learned. When you are constantly rehashing or thinking about past experiences with fear, anger, or feelings of injustice, you are not able to grow past them. Take action if there is action to be taken, and then let them go and recognize the lessons to be learned so that you may choose differently in the future.

The Work – Connecting and Loving Your Younger Self

In this exercise, you will ground yourself, come from a place of love and peace, and connect to yourself from the years past—your younger self, your teenage self, and your inner child. Throughout all the significant phases of your life, reconnect with that person and let them know how far you've made it. If you wish, you may play soft music in the background set to the heart chakra frequency of 639 Hz.

- Get into a comfortable position, sitting or lying down. Keep your neck and spine erect yet relaxed, soften your back and shoulders, and open your chest. Take a few moments to notice how your body is feeling and try to let go of any tension or tightness you're holding onto in your body, and relax deeper.
- Turn your awareness to your breathing. Take some time to just notice your breath, your inhales and exhales. Notice how and where your breath moves in you, out of you, and all around you.
- Start to slow your breathing, taking deeper, breaths. Think about and feel yourself filling your diaphragm and lungs with your breath, and allowing your breath to exhale naturally, letting go of what you no longer

need. As you breathe in, feel and picture yourself fill your body with breath, from the base of your torso, moving all the way up into your lungs and chest, and finally sending oxygen into your brain. Keep breathing deeply. You can also picture yourself pulling your breath up a tube that starts from your root chakra (the space by your perineum, in front of your tail bone, inside your body), and extends up in front of your spine, all the way up to the top of your head. Allow yourself to exhale naturally. Continue for five minutes.

- Let go of any forced breathing and turn your attention inward to your heart center, your heart chakra. This is the space inside your body, in the middle of your chest, behind your breastbone, and in front of your spine. Feel this space. Take a minute or two to just notice any sensations or experiences you may have. Keeping your awareness on this space, allow it to soften, relax, and open. Continue for five minutes.

- Bring into your heart center the intention to connect to your inner younger self—your inner child, your adolescent self, or younger adult self—one at a time. Have and feel the intention that you wish to connect to that younger self. Do your best to stay open to the experience. Engage all your senses.

- Invite your younger self to connect and speak with you. One at a time, invite a younger self (i.e., child, teenager, young adult, and other younger self from a significant phase in your life), to connect with you and repeat this part of the exercise for each. Let your younger self know that they are safe, loved, and it's going to be okay. Choose words and phrases that resonate and feel right for you, giving yourself the comfort and love that you needed. Ask them how they are feeling and reassure them lovingly if you get a response. Let them know they are perfect as they are and doing the best that they can. Comfort yourself with love. Do what feels right for you. Move on to the next younger self and repeat.

- When you've finished, come back to your heart center, feeling the energy and space in your heart chakra. Breathe deeply into this space and try to soften, relax, and open this space. When you feel ready, open your eyes. Take your time coming out of this exercise and then write your experience.
- Do your best not to judge your experience. This is an exercise you may come back to anytime.

> *Whenever I'm faced with a difficult decision, I ask myself, what would I do if I weren't afraid of making a mistake, feeling rejected, looking foolish or being alone? I know for sure that when you remove the fear, the answer you've been searching for, comes into focus. And as you walk into what you fear, you should know for sure, that your deepest trouble, can, if you're willing and open, produce your greatest strength.*
>
> Oprah Winfrey

Allow Fear to Show You the Way

Before you even started reading this book, you already had access to the best answer for yourself, but you were likely—and perhaps still are—afraid. That's okay. It's okay to be afraid of taking a risk or trying something new. It's okay to be worried about the unknown outcome or consequences. Take your time, but see if you can be with your fear instead of pushing it away. Let fear be your guide. Simply observe and feel. Notice what it is that you are reacting to, as there's something more for you there. When you find yourself reacting strongly to something, pause and observe, as there's something for you to explore in a deeper level. It may have triggered a pain that you have not allowed yourself to be with fully, accept, or let go. Allow fear to show you what you have been suppressing, what is fighting to surface and breakthrough, so that you can move past it. When you stop running away from your fears, the discomfort, challenges, and pain you'll face will help you become stronger, more resilient, and ultimately go further. Your best answers are sitting within—deep down, you already know it. You can break through the fear, move past it, and work through it. The decisions that feel right for you are waiting.

To answer with love is to move past the fear of failure or rejection and choose what you truly want. When you make your decisions with love instead of fear, your best answers are easy to discover. They may not be so easy to act upon, but you will grow and learn from the experience. Choosing an answer with love is making a decision that feels best and right for you, regardless of the potential unknowns and perceived consequences. Choosing answers rooted in fear will keep you in fear. It will keep you feeling low, so that you don't have to face the potential of not measuring up, losing, not being wanted, or being rejected. Choosing answers rooted in love means taking steps that enable you to feel lighter as you drop the fear, knowing that no matter what happens, you are enough.

To help you choose love instead of fear in your next steps and answers, you want to know that it's all going to be okay, and it will be. You are here to experience life, but you are more than your experiences. There will be challenges and losses, as well as opportunities and gains. There will be moments of joy and elation, along with moments of sadness and grief. Life is a series of experiences, and in the end, it will all be okay, because you are more than your experiences.

Start feeling more comfortable embracing the unknown in your answers by connecting within. There is a peace that is always inside of you, a light that cannot be shut off underneath the layers of trauma, fear, and hurt you're carrying, along with the walls you've put up. At your core, your essence is whole, no matter how broken you may think you are. By doing The Work—loving yourself, accepting, letting go, and being present—it will become easier to shed the layers of fear and doubt, and connect within to your essence, core, and light.

Know that choosing an answer based in love is never greedy, for love is infinite. You are never taking anything away from someone else when you choose with love. It doesn't matter what you may already have in your life, we are all deserving of experiencing more. You do not need to make yourself smaller, diminish yourself, or continue to force yourself to stay within a certain lane because you're worried about taking something away from others. When you choose love for yourself, there will be a ripple effect. Love is infinite. When we view our world and decisions as finite, we don't give ourselves the room to stretch and grow. Know that there is always more. Do what feels right for you in this moment. Choose love.

Let Go and Love Will Prevail

After being in our newly built house for a couple of years, one of the fence lines in our backyard started bothering me. We had torn down and rebuilt our house, and throughout the process, dealing with our neighbours was challenging, to say the least. Like many home construction and renovation projects, the process tested us. It was one of the most difficult experiences in our lives. The neighbours on either side of our property had both undertaken similar projects not too long prior to ours, and we felt we were easy going and amicable in the process, with neighbourly relations continuing as before with civility.

When it came to our project, it felt like the same courtesy was not extended. From the beginning, they made it clear they were going to be difficult, which was disappointing. By the end of the project, after two long, stressful years, we were finishing the backyard. At that point, I had expired my energy for the project and just wanted it done. One of our neighbours wanted to keep the fence line where it was, which was previously incorrectly built almost a foot into our property line, meaning they would keep the benefit of having and using our property in their backyard. This was a neighbour who had purposely flouted bylaws on more than one occasion to extend the reach of their property beyond the allowed means. The space that he wanted to keep on his side now would be between our fence and garage in the back lane way. Most people would've justifiably protested as it was a black and white case of simply putting the fence on the property line, as per the surveyed lot. However, I knew he would continue being contentious, and as I looked at the space, I knew we wouldn't be able to do much with it anyway. So, I said I didn't care. I just didn't want to deal with it anymore. My capacity for the project had been all spent. My husband reluctantly agreed after I told him I didn't want to fight about it, and the new fence was built partially on a diagonal line that cut into our property.

A couple of years later, from time to time, the fence line caught my eye, and I found myself getting irritated by it and by the whole situation with the neighbour. I felt myself being triggered just looking at it and was surprised that I was getting agitated. So, I meditated on it. Logically, I knew that there wasn't much we could do with that space anyway, and part of me felt that it was a bit silly to feel that any of us "owned" any land, as it really didn't belong to us, but rather to the earth. But still, it ate at me. So, I thought about what the lesson was for me here and honed in on forgiveness and letting go. I practiced that over and over again. And then, in one of my meditations, as I was asking for an answer on this issue and what to do, I got the answer: "Love will prevail." As I wrote this down in my journal, I found the words interesting and wasn't really sure what it all meant; however, I felt comforted by them and was finally able to let it go.

A couple of weeks later, we found out that the neighbour was selling their house. We felt that it was finally a good time to discuss moving the fence back to the property line and as he was moving, suddenly, he was nothing but amicable. He even helped move the fence back while making conversation with my husband like they were old friends and none of the past conflicts had ever happened. This was a complete reversal from two years prior. We finally got a straight fence on the property line, and I learned a lesson on forgiveness and letting go. My intuition also told me before anyone else even bought the house next door, that we'd have a great relationship with our new neighbours. I could just feel it. I was right. They're amazing, and we've become friends that spend time together. Love *did* prevail.

The Work – Explore Your Options

Consider your question and examine the possible answers and resulting scenarios. What are they? Use your journal to work through these prompts.

1. What are the best-case and worst-case scenarios for each option? Try not to let fear run away with your worst-case scenario. Be grounded and realistic. *(Side note: Remember from Chapter 3 that most people's worries didn't come true, and when they did, they were able to handle it better than anticipated.)*
2. Look at the worst-case scenarios, and create a brief action plan to counter, mitigate, or work through that

situation. Jot down some bullet points of what you would and could do in the worst-case scenario. Pause and notice how you feel as you consider the potential worst-case and your action plan resulting from it. Also consider how different the worst-case scenario is from where you are now and how you feel.

3. Look at the best-case scenarios and write down what that would look like, and how you would feel. How different is your best-case scenario from where you are now?

4. Now, imagine that you are walking down a path and reach a fork in the road with multiple paths to continue on. The path on the right side is the answer you choose with love, and the path on the left side is the answer you choose in fear. All the other permutations of answers are in between. Now, look further ahead into the future. What kind of life do you want to live? How do you want to feel in life? Which path will bring you closer to that space, that vision, that experience?

5. Now, consider if you only had a year left to live, which path would you choose? The reality is, as human beings, our bodies will all die someday, and we don't know exactly when our last breath will be. Perhaps we'll have one year, less than that, or a lot more. However, when you live for today, the present, making decisions with love can become much easier. How much longer will you wait until you make the best decisions for yourself?

Are you ready to choose with love?

And they queued up one by one
to say no thank you, this is not for me.
They left to find something more.
Left to reclaim what they had
unintentionally buried at the door.

CHAPTER 9

Trust Yourself

Trust yourself.
You already have the answers.

WHEN I TURNED thirty, I felt waves of sadness. No other birthday had bothered me before as I wasn't worried about aging; however, I hadn't accomplished all the goals I had planned and expected for myself by that point. Despite my financial and career success, I wasn't yet a mother, which pained me greatly. Around this time, I came across a quotation by Joseph Campbell that resonated and stayed with me: "We must be willing to let go of the life we've planned, so as to have the life that is waiting for us." I wrote it out on a chalkboard in my kitchen where it stayed up for quite some time.

For most of my career, I had a high paying, full-time corporate job, and in later years, I achieved the then standard "good" work-life balance of working 9am to 5pm, five days a week. I was trusted and respected at work and was identified by executives as having high potential to continue climbing the corporate ladder. However, I knew deep down that I didn't want to continue moving up into increasingly senior level roles because I didn't enjoy the environment, nor the work. My passion was helping others feel happier and healthier, yet I reasoned with myself that it was enough to do it on the side through mentorship, part-time yoga teaching, and volunteering with nonprofit organizations. The higher I progressed in the corporate environment, the more the job would center around corporate politics, pushing my own agenda, and navigating the organization through relationships instead of results. Up until that point, I'd always felt that I had succeeded based on the quality of my work and the results I produced. But to produce "results" at the next level in the environment I was in involved being able to spin my story and push my agenda, which essentially meant being good at corporate politics, which I detested. Despite it all, I told myself that I deserved to have an executive title, and so, I ignored my intuition and pushed on. In the span of a year, I was up for four different executive roles, all suited to my skills and qualifications, and for each one of them, I was told that while I was one of the top candidates, the role went to someone else who had less knowledge and experience, for external reasons that had nothing to do with me. I grew increasingly frustrated each time. Looking back, I now understand that I never got any of those roles because they truly weren't right for me. Not because I couldn't do them, but because that direction wasn't the best fit for *me*. I wouldn't have enjoyed them. This repeating obstacle was pushing me toward a new direction.

By forty, I had exited the corporate world completely, taking a big leap of faith into a whole new career path and leaving behind my expectations. I was wiser and understood that life doesn't always work out as planned, and that being present was the key to truly living. I had finally learned to be content in my journey, appreciating where I am. To be my best and just enjoy the process, which was and still can be a big mindset shift for me. With this, however, there is a deep knowing, a trust, and sense of peace, that all is and will be well. The future is unknown, and I am simply enjoying the present.

Enjoy the journey, for the present is a gift,
and the destination is just a moment in it.

The Path is Not Linear

I have learned that our paths in life are not linear. Regardless of what you may have believed growing up, there isn't a "right" order to live life. At times, you may feel like you're going in circles, zig zagging from highs to lows, stagnating, or moving forward only to take steps backward—but you keep going. What you may see as a challenge, setback, or obstacle can turn out to be a steppingstone in a new direction. A difficult situation may lead to something that wasn't even in your realm of thinking, which later becomes an experience you are deeply grateful for as it guided you in a new direction. For example, it may sound crazy, but I am truly grateful for getting that unexpected cancer diagnosis, as it forced me to stop in my tracks and start being, instead of just doing. There are always opportunities for you to learn and grow if you can recognize them.

On your journey, you may be frustrated as it doesn't feel like you're progressing when you're in the daily grind. But know that progress doesn't always look like a straight line ascending on a line graph. If you look closely, you'll see that there are dips, valleys, and ascents that may look like a series of hills. But if you step back, zoom out, and look at your journey from a broader and higher perspective, you will see that there is a gradual progression of ascension. You no longer see the dips and valleys that led to the ascents, just the broader trajectory of rising. You are rising. Even if it feels very slow, you are rising.

Pay attention to the experiences that are repeating themselves. Notice if you keep encountering similar challenges or obstacles in your path, as there's a reason for it. What do you need to learn to not repeat this obstacle again? The next time you come across a similar challenge, what is the new perspective you're bringing? Is there something you need to accept and let go of to move forward? There is no losing when you are learning.

Start taking small steps toward your answer. Thinking of trying a new career? Perhaps take a course within that field while doing your day job. Thinking about moving? Visit the place(s) you have in mind, explore, and talk to some locals, or take a vacation there for a few days. Thinking about leaving your relationship? Take some time apart. Assess how you feel, and talk to them about how they feel afterwards. Start taking small steps toward your answer until you're ready to take bigger ones, and before long, when you turn around to see how far you've come, you'll be amazed. It all starts with one step. One step can be as simple as a thought or an intention. It can be as life changing as saying "no" instead of "yes", or "yes" instead of "no". Start taking steps in the direction that *feels* right for you, and that is where your best answers lay.

Focus on What You Can Control, Let Go of The Rest

Focus on what you can control and let go of the rest. Fixating on feelings and experiences outside your control only serves to weigh you down in your journey. Let go. Make the decisions that feel right for you, do the best that you can, and let go of the rest. You cannot control other people's perceptions of your outputs. Their reactions are their own; you are not responsible for them. Act with love in your decisions and reactions, towards others and yourself. As you let go, you allow life to unfold without resistance. The less you resist, the more you will flow. Allow your answers to unfold in front of you.

After going through all The Work, steps, and exercises outlined in the chapters, if you still don't know what direction to take, what the right answer is for you, what answer *feels best*, I encourage you to give yourself space and time. Maybe it's not your time yet to answer the question and you'll feel differently when you revisit the question in the near future. As you wait, allow life to unfold naturally; do not resist. Keep doing The Work, and pay attention to the messages and signs that resonate with you.

Change is inevitable. Nothing ever stays the same. Sometimes, a situation that feels difficult or hopeless will find a way of working out on its own, without your intervention, but aided by your intention. As you continue with The Work, consciously allow your life to unfold naturally, without resistance. Make decisions that feel right for you and let go of what you can't control. Simply let life unfold. Allow it to take you to where you need to be, at that moment. If you feel content where you are, you don't need to pressure yourself into a decision. Keep looking for the signs. Follow the breadcrumbs that are being left for you. The universe is always speaking to you; you just need to know how to pay attention.

As you continue with your inner work, you will feel a pull toward the direction of change that feels right. Don't be afraid to step out of your comfort zone. You can start gradually with the smallest steps. An intention is a step. Changing one word in the way you think or speak is a step. Decisions don't need to be made in one fell swoop. You can start taking small steps toward the direction that feels right, even if you're not 100% sure about it. As you inch your way forward, your path will become clearer.

If you've gone through all the steps and are ready for change but there isn't an answer that truly feels best for you, then jump. Go in the direction that may scare you—the one that you would take if you knew that it would all work out, without fear. Try it out. Start taking steps in that direction and see what happens. See how you feel. If you're meant to change direction later, you'll feel it. Embarking on your journey in one direction doesn't mean that you have to stay on that same road forever. Sometimes, we take one direction or path in our journey to get to the next step, the next fork in the road. And that is enough.

Tune into Yourself

Like the quotations that stayed with me, what words, sentences, numbers, images, and sounds have stood out for you? Notice what you notice as those messages are for you. What has lingered in your mind after seeing, hearing, or experiencing them? The universe, your guides, and your soul are constantly sharing messages that you can access if you learn to listen, recognize the signs, and tune in. These messages can guide you and ultimately point to the answers within.

Trust in the answers that come from your inner wisdom—the answers you feel when you connect within to your heart center. This is where you can access the best answers for yourself and get confirmation whether an action is right for you. There can be different voices in your head, but only your divine connection in your heart, so, trust your heart for your greatest guidance. The more you can connect to your heart, your body, and your inner wisdom or intuition, the more the answers will become clearer to you.

The right path for you is the one that *feels right* for you. When you can remove the distractions from your mind chatter, stress, and worries, you will find that the answers that allow you to flow effortlessly may feel best. Just as water will always find the path of least resistance, your heart will know the best path for you that will allow you to flow to your destination.

Trust Yourself

When I was interviewing for a job at the last corporation I worked at, they asked me where I saw myself in the future. I told them that I planned to stay at the company for about four years, and then would leave to start my own business. It wasn't a pre-conceived answer. I intuitively said what felt right at that time. I was right. Somehow, I knew that it would be my last corporate job, and that afterward, I would work for myself. Uncoincidentally, I received the cancer diagnosis after working there for four years, and then left my job on medical leave. Months later, when I was cleared to go back to work, I knew in my gut that I couldn't return, as the corporate world was no longer for me. I didn't know exactly what path I would take next, but I had a knowing—a feeling—that it would all work out for the best, and that I'd have all my needs fulfilled and more. While I didn't know exactly what I would do, I knew that it would involve helping others live healthier and happier lives, and I wanted to work for myself. I turned my attention inward to myself, took time to heal, meditate, practice yoga, journal, connect, and ultimately love myself more while working on letting go of what no longer served me. My faith in myself grew stronger, and I had no doubt that I would well surpass the income I made before, simply working to uplift others. I told my husband all this, and he said, "How do you know?" I paused for a moment and replied, "I just know." A younger me would've been frightened to leave the safety of a steady corporate job and venture into the unknown. With no set plans, many would question how it could all be achieved. But something inside me knew this was going to happen. I finally trusted in the unknown. To have doubts, negative thoughts, and worries wouldn't help me; it would only help attract more of that energy to me. So, I trusted my gut and stayed focused on feeling happy, grateful, and healthy. I worked on breaking down my limiting beliefs and replacing them with gratitude, joy, and self-love. I was living in the present, with no regrets, and with my arms wide open for the future.

Many of you may already know the right answer for yourself, but you don't trust it or yourself, so, you question and analyze it over and over again, from all angles. You may look for external validation from others to confirm whether what you're thinking is right or wrong. You look to outside sources for guidance on your most personal questions. Deep down, however, you already hold the answer. Trust yourself. It may be that you have an inkling of the answer but you're too afraid to admit it, face it, or make that choice. However, no one knows you or your situation better than yourself. You are your own best teacher. You don't need a psychic to tell you the answer. And it's okay to not be ready to face the answer yet. Take your time. Work on building yourself up with love and self-care, and when the time is right, you'll be ready. Keep working on all the steps and exercises. Understand them, try them out, and consistently work through them to know that you'll always be able to access the answers you need to any of your life's major questions. There is no need for that external validation. Trust in yourself. Connect to your heart center, and you will feel what is best for you. That doesn't mean it is the easy answer. You may not be ready to accept it or act on it yet, and that's okay. Be gentle with yourself. This is a process. The Work and steps outlined in the book—meditation, journaling and self-love—will help you get there when you're ready. However, know that the answers you're looking for are not found outside of you, but within.

Trust that while you may not know exactly how things will turn out, that things are unfolding at the right time, and in the right space for you. Trust in the unknown. To doubt is to give into fear, which leads to more stress and anxiety that doesn't assist you. Do the best that you can, make decisions that feel right for you, and then let go.

My hope is that this book helps you on your path to finding those answers. If you are reading this now, you are on your way, even if it may not feel like it yet.

Change Your Inner World and Your Outer World Will Change

When you change your inner world, your outer world will change as well. When you put yourself first, love and care for yourself, give yourself time and space, do things that bring you joy, allow yourself to feel it all and express it, listen, and learn from yourself, the answers will come. They are waiting for you. The steps in this book are simply to help you find them and have the confidence to act.

There is no one better person equipped to make the right decision for your life than yourself. No one knows you better. You *can* make the right decisions, even if they are tough. Many of you probably started reading this book with a question or two in mind, thinking it would help you with landing on the best answer, and I sincerely hope that it did. I believe though, that you had that answer inside you all along. My hope is that this book and the practices outlined in these pages helped you bring it out, voice it, and accept it, which can often be the bigger struggle. After all this, know that the answer is never far as it is always within you. You have the answer, and you are the answer.

When the answer becomes clearer, you may feel relief and you may also feel scared. If taking the next step toward the answer is easy, that is wonderful. If taking the next step toward the answer is scary, that is perfectly fine. It's not always going to be easy, but it will always feel right to follow your truth. You don't need to look into the distance at the finish line, just focus on the next step. After all, there is no final finish line, for at the end of each journey is a new beginning. So, be present. You will be pleasantly surprised at how things turn out when you're not worried about the future and focused on the present with an open mind and heart. As you go forward, remember that your best answers lay within. You can do this. Trust yourself, and know that love is always the answer.

In the end, answers are easy, but action takes work. If you've read up to here, then you've taken action already. If you tried any of The Work, exercises, and practices, you took action. You took another step in your journey. Now ask yourself, "What action will I take next?"

RESOURCES

For information on classes (including meditation and yoga), events, and content that Jane Lee offers, please sign up for her email list and visit her website at **www.PureLeeJane.com**

The following is a list of resources that Jane Lee has used and found helpful in her personal journey.

Books:

- A New Earth—Eckhart Tolle
- Becoming Supernatural—Dr. Joe Dispenza
- Lovingkindness: The Revolutionary Art of Happiness—Sharon Salzberg
- Power vs. Force—David R. Hawkins
- Radical Remissions: Surviving Cancer Against All Odds—Kelly Turner
- The Brain That Changes Itself—Norman Doidge
- The Brain's Way of Healing—Norman Doidge
- The Four Agreements—Don Miguel Ruiz
- The Power is Within You—Louise Hay
- The Power of Now—Eckhart Tolle

Meditation:

- Joe Dispenza – www.drjoedispenza.com
- Mindfulness Based Stress Reduction (MBSR) – multiple MBSR courses available globally
- The Chopra App – Guided Meditations and well-being app

Podcasts:

- Impact the World with Lee Harris
- Oprah's Super Soul Sundays

ENDNOTES

Chapter 2: Connect to Your Body & Intuition

[1] https://www.dailymail.co.uk/news/article-1190759/Mighty-mothers-superhuman-strength-lift-1-400kg-car-run-schoolboy.html; https://en.wikipedia.org/wiki/Hysterical_strength

[2] https://www.wrdw.com/2021/05/31/boy-7-swims-for-an-hour-to-save-family-after-boating-mishap

[3] Bechara, A., Damasio, A. R., Damasio, H., Anderson, S. W. "Insensitivity to future consequences following damage to human prefrontal cortex," Cognition Volume 50, Issues 1-3, April–June 1994, Pages 7-15.

[4] Kandasamy, N. et al. "Interoceptive Ability Predicts Survival on a London Trading Floor," Scientific Reports, 6, 32986; 2016

Chapter 3: Making Space for Your Answers with Meditation

[5] https://www.singlecare.com/blog/news/anxiety-statistics/

[6] https://www.nimh.nih.gov/health/statistics/any-anxiety-disorder

[7] Vahratian A, Blumberg SJ, Terlizzi EP, Schiller JS. "Symptoms of Anxiety or Depressive Disorder and Use of Mental Health Care Among Adults During the COVID-19 Pandemic — United States, August 2020–February 2021," MMWR Morbidity and Mortality Weekly Report 2021; 70: 490–494.

[8] Lucas S. LaFreniere, Michelle G. Newman, "Exposing Worry's Deceit: Percentage of Untrue Worries in Generalized Anxiety Disorder Treatment," Behavior Therapy, Volume 51, Issue 3, 2020, Pages 413-423.

ENDNOTES

[9] Borkovec, Thomas & Hazlett-Stevens, Holly & Diaz, M.L.. (1999). "The Role of Positive Beliefs about Worry in Generalized Anxiety Disorder and its Treatment," Clinical Psychology & Psychotherapy. 6. 126 - 138.

[10] https://www.mindful.org/jon-kabat-zinn-defining-mindfulness

[11] https://www.healthline.com/nutrition/12-benefits-of-meditation

[12] https://www.simplypsychology.org/brain-plasticity.html

[13] Lazar SW, Kerr CE, Wasserman RH, et al. "Meditation experience is associated with increased cortical thickness," Neuroreport. 2005;16(17):1893-1897.

[14] ibid

[15] Gotink RA, Meijboom R, Vernooij MW, Smits M, Hunink MG. "8-week Mindfulness Based Stress Reduction induces brain changes similar to traditional long-term meditation practice - A systematic review," Brain Cogn. 2016 Oct;108:32-41.; Goldin PR, Gross JJ. "Effects of mindfulness-based stress reduction (MBSR) on emotion regulation in social anxiety disorder," Emotion. 2010;10(1):83-91.

[16] Holzel BK, Carmody J, Evans KC, Hoge EA, Dusek JA, Morgan L, et al. "Stress reduction correlates with structural changes in the amygdala," Social Cognitive and Affective Neuroscience. 2010;5(1):11–17.

[17] Holzel BK, Carmody J, Evans KC, Hoge EA, Dusek JA, Morgan L, et al. "Stress reduction correlates with structural changes in the amygdala," Social Cognitive and Affective Neuroscience. 2010;5(1):11–17; Farb NA, Segal ZV, Mayberg H, Bean J, McKeon D, Fatima Z, Anderson AK, "Attending to the present: mindfulness meditation reveals distinct neural modes of self-reference," Social Cognitive and Affective Neuroscience. 2007 Dec; 2(4):313-22; Goldin PR, Gross JJ, "Effects of mindfulness-based stress reduction (MBSR) on emotion regulation in social anxiety disorder," Emotion. 2010 Feb; 10(1):83-91.

[18] https://www.health.harvard.edu/staying-healthy/understanding-the-stress-response

Chapter 4: Journaling

[19] Karen A. Baikie, Kay Wilhelm, "Emotional and physical health benefits of expressive writing," Advances in Psychiatric Treatment, Cambridge University Press, Jan 2, 2018

[20] https://www.health.harvard.edu/healthbeat/giving-thanks-can-make-you-happier

Chapter 5: Address Your Blocks

[21] Garrison KA, Zeffiro TA, Scheinost D, Constable RT, Brewer JA. "Meditation leads to reduced default mode network activity beyond an active task," Cognitive, Affective, & Behavioral Neuroscience. 2015;15(3):712-720.

Chapter 7: Dream Interpretation

[22] https://mossdreams.com/about/
[23] Sander van der Linden, "The Science Behind Dreaming," Scientific American, Jul 26, 2011

ACKNOWLEDGEMENTS

DEEP APPRECIATION AND thanks to my family, friends, students, clients, and all those who have encouraged me in my journey. Thank you to all of the teachers who have influenced and impacted my life and work. Most of all, I recognize that I would not be where I am without the love and support of my mom, earth angel daughter Evelyn, and my love, Dave. Thank you for lifting me up, and shining so brightly to help light my path.

And thank you, dear reader. I am grateful that you chose to read this book and spend some of your precious time with my words and energy. Just as those above have been lights in my journey, I am grateful if I can be one of the many lights that illuminate yours.

Manufactured by Amazon.ca
Bolton, ON

28701602R00118